A **Brief Introduction** to **Sigmund Freud's Psychoanalysis** *and His Enduring Legacy*

A **Brief Introduction** to **Sigmund Freud's Psychoanalysis** *and His Enduring Legacy*

Sander M. Abend M.D.

IPBOOKS.net
International Psychoanalytic Books

Contents

Foreword by Owen Renik ix

CHAPTER I 1
Introduction

CHAPTER II 5
Freud's Early Years and the Focus on Trauma

CHAPTER III 23
Freud: The Middle Years: Topographic Theory and
Transference

CHAPTER IV 35
Freud: The Late Years: Structural Theory and the Rise
of the Ego

CHAPTER V 53
The Growth of Freudian Psychoanalysis After Freud's
Death

CHAPTER VI 61
Freud's Enduring Legacy

References 77

Foreword by Owen Renik

Simply put, this book should be required reading for anyone wishing to study psychoanalysis. Here are three good reasons: First, Abend applies his considerable psychoanalytic scholarship, as well as his long clinical experience, to making a thorough, careful, and complete presentation of Freud's essential ideas—which is something not to be taken for granted: important elements of Freud's work are all too often misunderstood or overlooked elsewhere.

Abend never talks down to the reader; he does not shy away from detail and complexity. At the same time, he makes his presentation clearly and with a deceptive simplicity, so that it is always easy reading.

Second, Abend's format is to trace the historic unfolding of Freud's thinking. This is, again, a difficult task which is rarely accomplished with complete success, because of the many twists and turns Freud's thinking took, not to mention the incompletions and even contradictions that Freud left standing. Abend gracefully unties the knots and connects the dots, permitting the reader to appreciate Freud's consistent ulterior logic.

Third, Abend makes the well judged choice to take up only those developments in psychoanalysis following Freud that have remained directly in line with Freud's thought. It is, of course, very much in keeping with the psychoanalytic understanding that what comes first has a profound influence upon what comes after to make as complete as possible a study of the elaboration that has taken place of the principles originally articulated by Freud before studying divergences and departures from those principles. As Abend emphasizes, judgments about what is and what is not truly Freudian are bound to be controversial. Confronted with the necessity to make difficult choices, Abend's distinguished scholarship shines in his discussion of post-Freudian Freudianism. He offers neither too much nor too little, and shows that it is all of a piece.

Abend has done justice to Freud's enduring legacy. Readers of this book are given the very valuable opportunity to learn what that legacy is and why it has endured.

CHAPTER I

Introduction

Sigmund Freud was securely established as a productive medical researcher when, approaching middle age, he made a decision that would prove to be of profound significance, not only for him personally, but for the world at large. He chose to leave his comfortable academic post and to begin a private practice in neurology, specializing in treating the then common ailments that would soon thereafter come to be known as "neuroses." In this new endeavor he was, of course, seeking to learn how best to relieve his patients' distress. He also could not help but continue to make use of the skills he had employed during his years of research. He utilized his exceptional powers of careful observation, combined with his restless intellectual curiosity and his tendency to try to organize his findings into conceptual schemata. While he was functioning as a clinical neurologist, his aim was to better understand the underlying causes of those neurotic ailments, and to systematize their treatment. The result was his development of the method he soon came to call "psychoanalysis." His exploratory efforts led him, in the course of his clinical work, to attempt to construct and organize what turned out to be a highly original, quite unique visualization of the workings of the human mind.

Today we can see with hindsight that his achievement soon gave birth to a great variety of more-or-less similar treatment methods, many of which also adopted the same title, that is "psychoanalysis." In fact, it seems altogether fair to say that Freud's new treatment may be regarded as the true parent of the entire panoply of so-called "talking treatments" that are still firmly ensconced in our therapeutic armamentarium. Moreover, his continuing attention to trying to uncover and understand the complex workings of the unconscious mind gave rise to a body of theory that also came to be known by the same designation, "psychoanalysis."

I shall not attempt to identify, describe or evaluate the broad spectrum of psychoanalytic variations with which we are confronted today. The interested reader can readily find expositions of them by practitioners and scholars who are immersed in each, and are thus far more qualified than I to do them justice. Instead, my aim in what follows is to concentrate exclusively upon the work of Sigmund Freud himself, and to summarize and explain it in such a fashion that an audience of educated persons can better grasp Freud's enduring legacy, the evolution of his ideas, and their complexity. I am convinced that an accurate comprehension of his achievements can best be attained by following the emergence and modification of his formulations in historical sequence, His ideas changed substantially as he gained more clinical experience and as he interacted with a growing band of followers and rivals.

In the past it was often proposed that a reliable assessment of Freud's work and ideas could only be obtained through the experience of being an analytic patient, and/or by gaining some experience in practicing his technique with patients. The reasoning behind this notion was that psychoanalysis began as an empirical study, and it has long been considered a truism that clinical evidence is the most reliable support for, and convincing proof of, this study. Freud himself was fond of quoting Charcot, the famous French neurologist with whom Freud studied for a time, to the effect that, "…theory is fine, but it does not change the facts."

The reader must keep in mind that in Freud's time, the belief was prevalent that qualified persons could be capable of clearly ascertaining "facts," and similarly, to accurately evaluate both truth and reality. Such relative clarity and certainty are by no means thought so easily attainable in our present intellectual climate. Consequently, it is not at all surprising to contemporary thinkers that what may have appeared to be a very direct and pragmatic approach to evaluation in Freud's time does not hold true today. In psychoanalysis, as in other domains, it is by no means a simple matter to determine precisely what constitutes the "facts" in question. Furthermore, we are compelled to admit that exactly what makes up valid clinical evidence is not easy to ascertain, either. Even practitioners who hold to compatible theories and techniques may arrive at varying interpretations of the clinical data.

Thus the would-be student who does not have direct personal experience of psychoanalysis, from either end of the couch, is obliged to rely upon the writings and lectures of others for information. It seems to me worthwhile to offer them one cautionary note: in considering any exposition of psychoanalytic theory, one ought not to be too impressed by elegance of phrase or ingenuity of speculation. Psychoanalytic propositions and theories will no doubt at some time come to be measured by their coherence with the neuro-scientific discoveries; but that time is not yet upon us.

I intend to focus upon the finding and theories of Sigmund Freud alone, merely mentioning a few important refinements and clarifications of his corpus which emerged in certain of his followers in the decades after his death in 1939. My purpose then is merely to describe and clarify Freud's particular contributions, and, in conclusion, to make note of some elements of them that I think may constitute his enduring legacy. In so doing, I shall draw upon my career-long immersion in the study of his work. I have read, taught and written about Freud's discoveries and contributions, and I have practiced my interpretation of his methodology for many years. Mine is not the only version of Freudian psychoanalysis, and I do not claim to hold a unique position of expertise. I will, however, make every effort to be faithful to his writings in my brief summary of his career and output, which follows this intro-duction. I will endeavor, in so far as I can, to permit Sigmund Freud to speak for himself.

CHAPTER II

Freud's Early Years and the Focus on Trauma

Freud once called himself "one of those who have disturbed the sleep of the world," and for good reason. The cumulative impact of his findings about the nature of mind and consciousness was in his time, and for that matter still is, quite upsetting to mankind's collective self-esteem. This is so because the essence of his discoveries challenges our most fundamental and comfortable notions about ourselves. We are accustomed to believe that most of us are essentially rational and sensible beings, whose unique form of intelligence enables us to occupy a special place in the order of nature. To be sure that is to some degree quite true. Yet, as a consequence of Freud's discoveries, we have been obliged to recognize that the practical, everyday reliability of our way of thinking and of our store of memories, perceptions, feelings—even our control of our behavior—are by no means always realistic, reasonable, or sensible. We are not, after all, so much masters of our fate as we are actors in personal dramas of whose true nature we have but the faintest grasp.

Writers, philosophers, scientists, and other thinkers in the West, from at least the time of the Greeks onward, have been able to appreciate that mankind's independent self-knowledge and self-determination are clearly a comfortable myth. That said, not all acknowledge that this misunderstanding of our abilities, thinking and behavior does not merely burden certain unfortunate individuals, but applies to all times and to all people. Sigmund Freud's contribution to this unsettling revelation was achieved by his unprecedented approach to the study of mental functioning, which pointed out the limitations of our conscious awareness in a crystalline and manifestly systematic fashion. His work revealed that even our very best conscious efforts at self-knowledge are invariably subject to distortion, and are incomplete and self-deceiving at best. He demonstrated that many of the thought processes that determine our judgment and activity are powerfully affected by ideas, images, memories and even fantasies. These occupy a place in our mind which is not only outside of our awareness, but is also in large measure inaccessible to it. Furthermore, he was in time able to show that this is the case precisely because so many of these processes are, or would be, unwelcome to our conscious selves. No wonder, then, that he came to think of himself as a profound disruptor of our comfortable self-assurance. His work was a journey into uncharted realms, many of which well deserve the poetic warning, "Here there be dragons."

I shall try to tell the story of his career in a sequential fashion, emphasizing the gradual accumulation of his clinical observations that led to the consequent changes in and clarifications of his theoretical propositions and conclusions. It is important for the reader to keep in mind that as Freud gained experience he often, although not always, felt obliged to modify his theoretical understanding. Therefore, it follows that any random, non-chronological study of his publications is almost bound to be misleading to those interested in understanding his ideas.

Freud was born in Freiburg in 1856, and moved with his family to Vienna when he was four years old. From the beginning he was a brilliant student, and was thought of as one who was destined for high achievement, not least of all in his own estimation.. After completing his studies in medicine, he found a place in the laboratory of the eminent physiologist Dr. Ernst Brucke, whereupon he aspired to make great discoveries. He was fully engaged in research, and in fact did significant work on aphasia and also on the anesthetic properties of cocaine, among other foci of interest. According to Freud himself, he felt obliged to leave academia, where he was very content, in order to earn a better livelihood, thus to facilitate his plans for marriage and future. Clinical practice was potentially much more lucrative than his research career, and so he commenced this new endeavor, choosing to specialize in treating diseases of the nervous system. To advance his knowledge, he arranged to spend a year in Paris (1885) at the famous Salpetriere, under the aegis of the world-famous professor J. A. Charcot.

The latter's fame rested (and still does) on his detailed exploration of "hysteria," unique for his day, which demonstrated for the first time that the paralytic and anesthetic symptoms common to sufferers from this malady simply did not correspond to any known neurologic pathways. Freud was impressed by Charcot's findings, but not satisfied with his explanation that there must exist some unspecified and undetected degeneration of the nervous system in hysterics. In passing, let us note that at the time hysteria was an ill-defined diagnosis applied to individuals displaying a variety of symptoms, not only paralyses and focal anesthesias, but also various postural and gait abnormalities and speech disturbances. All of these, appearing either singly or in combination, were of a mysterious and dramatic nature. It was believed by the less politically enlightened medical establishment of the era that women were primarily, if not exclusively, subject to such disorders; hence the perhaps unintentionally discriminatory label, which is derived from the Greek word for the uterus.

Freud returned to Vienna, eager to share his recently acquired knowledge and his curiosity about what might be the true cause of these disturbances. He was disappointed to find that the local medical community was not especially interested in his reports of Charcot's work. He was, however, himself quite interested in treating such patients, of whom there were quite a number. The accepted modes of therapy at that time included the use of hypnosis for both diagnostic and therapeutic ends. The late stages of treatment often utilized hypnotic suggestion as a tool. Freud later wrote that he also employed hypnosis in order to inquire about the origin of his patients' symptoms. In that effort he followed in the footsteps of Dr. Joseph Breuer, who had used this unusual application of hypnotic technique in the successful treatment of a complicated case of hysteria.

Freud journeyed once again to France to learn more about hypnosis from doctors Liebault and Bernheim, who were at that time the outstanding authorities on hypnotic phenomena. Thus armed, he returned to Vienna and was able to persuade Breuer to collaborate with him on the treatment of cases of hysteria. Together they wrote the now historically famous 1895 monograph on the subject, entitled *Studies on Hysteria*.

In this work they outlined what they came to call the "cathartic method" of treatment. It was so named because their investigation of the origins of patients' symptoms led at times to an outpouring of painful memories and emotions, which were often followed by a certain degree of relief of their suffering. Although one some-times hears even today of catharsis as a modality of psychological treatment, in truth it is more properly to be regarded as a some-what naive forerunner of what was soon to become clinical psychoanalysis. This is so because, as Freud soon came to see from his further work with such patients, while cathartic eruptions of feelings and memories might well bring about some immediate relief, this result often proved to be only temporary. He was obliged to conclude that something further was necessary in order to solidify these transient advances.

The answer would prove to lie in the extraordinary "next step" he conceived, that of attributing coherent explanatory meaning to the patients' material: that is to say, the comments, emotions and activities expressed and revealed when his patients focused on telling him about the origin of their symptoms. A new era in the treatment of what later on proved to be psychological disorders commenced with Freud's realization that the symptoms of his patients' ailments turned out to have very direct symbolic connections to their buried thoughts, memories and feelings. The germ of what was soon to become psychoanalysis was, in fact, quite literally a matter of applying analysis to what was unearthed by his exploration of their psyches

Freud was trained neither as a psychologist nor as a philosopher; he was a medical doctor and a researcher, and thus a careful scientific observer. Even more important, he possessed the courage and the confidence to stick to his conclusions about what he learned from his patients, even in the face of what he found to be the obvious disbelief, and often derision, of his medical community. This stubbornness soon proved to be a necessary stance, because of the problem his colleagues had accepting the surprising nature of what he was discovering about the roots of his patients' troubles. In all his patients Freud encountered what he considered to be unmistakable evidence that their recollections of the upsetting experiences which lay at the heart of their problems, always turned out to be traumas of a sexual nature. Much later, Freud wrote (1925, pg. 24) "I was not prepared for this conclusion and my expectation played no part in it, for I had begun my investigation of neurotics quite unsuspectingly." Needless to say, this surprising and disconcerting finding was rejected by his colleagues, and even Breuer was so dismayed by it that he quickly ended their collaboration.

For the moment, let us step aside from this well-known cultural upheaval and its ramifications, in order to return to the important evolution of Freud's inspired technical innovations and their consequences. A few thinkers today believe that this dimension of Freud's ultimate legacy is at least as important and influential as his sexual findings would prove to be.

As I have said earlier, Freud abandoned the use of hypnosis when he realized that the relief it sometimes produced was only temporary, and thus he no longer could depend upon hypnosis as a tool for exploring his patients' memories. He began instead to employ rather insistent suggestion as a way to get patients to recall the forgotten traumatic moments that had subsequently given rise to their symptoms. In short order, he learned that it was not necessary to urge them to focus on the subject of their symptoms in order to gain access to those memories. Instead, he discovered that he merely had to encourage them to allow their conscious minds to roam without any specific aim or focused subject. He also asked them to report aloud to him whatever occurred to them, urging them to speak without editing or censoring their utterances. Thus was born the now famous and familiar modality that has ever since been called "free association." It became a tool of unparalleled value in exploring the mind, and thereby of clarifying its hidden intricacies. With the use of this new technique, Freud opened a previously undreamed-of way of bringing about relief to those who suffered from painful psychological symptoms.

The key to this inspired technical breakthrough was Freud's conviction that these so-called "free associations" were in fact anything but free. Their seemingly random patterns were invariably determined by whatever matters were active at that moment in the unconscious stratum of each patient's mind, or so Freud came to believe. It is difficult to exaggerate the importance that this conjecture about the vital role of unconscious mental activity was to occupy, not only in Freud's subsequent career, but in the psychological thinking of generations of thinkers who followed him. By utilizing his newly developed technique, Freud soon came to appreciate that the recollections which emerged as indicators of the root causes of his patients' symptoms were always subjects that were quite distressing to them. It became clear to Freud that it was precisely this feature of those memories that explained why they had been buried beneath the surface of consciousness. Furthermore, they were not at all easy to bring out into the light of those persons' conscious awareness. He coined the term "resistance" to label the force within each patient's mind that vigorously battled against remembering these traumatic events. In time, the same term was also applied to what Freud came to observe as the patients' seemingly automatic need to oppose the analyst's efforts to bring this important but disturbing material to their conscious attention.

This ingenious, intricate conception of the workings of the mind in his neurotic patients led Freud in time to formulate what has become known as the theory of "repression." This term stands for his growing conclusion that a balance of opposing forces was at work in all such cases. On the one side were the troublesome memories and ideas associated with the symptoms of illness. On the other side was a powerful psychological force, its exact nature as yet unspecified, which sought to prevent the emergence of those disturbing traumatic items into consciousness. Thus was born the theory of mental conflict as a dominant descriptive feature of neurotic illness.

It was also Freud's belief that the unconscious contents of repression in each patient, which could not emerge into awareness in undisguised, recognizable form because of the defending blockage, could in some circumstances express themselves in distorted forms, which constituted the symptoms of the neurosis. This explanation of the mechanism of symptom formation seemed quite logical to him at the time. Its importance lay in the gradual shift in Freud's view of the way therapy was supposed to work. Earlier, he had believed that the uncovering of the buried contents thought to be causing the symptoms resulted in a presumptively healing catharsis of the painful memories and emotions. His view of the importance of repression and mental conflict led him to shift emphasis to the specific task of identifying and overcoming the patients' resistance. He concluded that this work, when successful, could clear the way for the traumatic roots of the illness to come to the surface of consciousness and thus be recognized and understood. In time, this therapeutic procedure could reduce harmful effects on an afflicted person's well being, or so Freud had come to think.

For the would-be therapist, this new focus made the work of relieving neurotic suffering much more laborious and time-consuming. I have thus condensed Freud's historic initial struggle to clarify the underlying explanatory factors of neurotic symptoms, and his gradual refinement of a therapeutic template for their relief, into a few sentences. This succinct summary hardly does justice to the time, effort and imagination that was required to reach this point in the development of psychoanalysis. The conceptual breakthrough clarifying the theory—that the surface phenomena of neurotic symptoms could be decoded into the unconscious images, memories and thoughts that produced them—was of profound significance. It can perhaps be seen as parallel to his great discovery that the manifest material of dreams, as mysterious as they, too, seemed to be, could also be decoded to reveal the underlying thoughts that produced them.

The notion that our dreams have meaning is, to be sure, centuries older than Freud's work on the subject of dream interpretation. Wise men, seers, psychics and shamans of every era, at least since Biblical times, and probably even earlier, have provided interpretations to interested individuals. Joseph and his fabled interpretation for the Pharaoh of Egypt is probably one of the most famous and familiar instances. Having dreams predict some future event, as in that example, was apparently common. As far as we know, "magical" intuition, perhaps aided by astute political awareness, seems to have been utilized by those interpreters of dreams. Freud's approach to the task was, in contrast, uniquely systematic. He regarded the images, events and sounds that constituted what he called the "manifest content" of dreams (or, in other words, what the dreamer could recall and report of them once awake) as akin to the symptoms that appeared as the manifestations of neurotic illness. He was convinced that in both these sets of data—the phenomena of symptoms and the imagery of dreams—the analyst-interpreter could uncover the underlying unconscious thoughts that were the source material. After an exhaustive application of his free- association technique to the dreams supplied by some of his patients, as well as some of his own dreams, he published a monumental book, *The Interpretation of Dreams*, in 1900. Forever after, he continued to regard this volume as his masterpiece, offering several subsequent revisions to further clarify some particulars therein. In fact, this book is still studied by students more than a century after it first appeared.

The book opens with a thorough review of the existing literature on dreams and dreaming, and then proceeds to set forth in great detail what Freud observed and concluded about the construction of dreams. He takes into account the mental state in operation during dreaming sleep, and applies his free-association method for decoding the imagery of dreams into the thoughts they expressed. The book is still readily available to anyone who is interested, and even a selective perusal of its contents will present vivid examples of dreams and their interpretation.

Perhaps most startling to readers of that time was Freud's assertion that dreams always embodied the disguised fulfillment of an unconscious wish. He thought that the motive for the illogical surface forms of the dreams was the underlying unconscious wishes that stimulated their creation, which were not acceptable to the dreamers' conscious minds and therefore had to be disguised! The parallel to his discoveries about symptom formation are quite evident.

For purposes of illustration, I shall insert an abbreviated version of one of the sample dreams from Freud's book (pp. 146ff). He is quoting a female patient who reported during a session a dream she thought might contradict Freud's assertion that dreams invariably express the fulfillment of a wish in the dreamer's unconscious mind. She cited the following dream: *"I wanted to give a supper party, but I had nothing in the house but a little smoked salmon. I thought I would go out and buy something but remembered then that it was Sunday afternoon and all the shops would be shut. Next I tried to ring up some caterers, but the telephone was out of order. So I had to abandon my wish to give a supper party."*

Freud's description of his analysis begins by stating that the patient's husband had remarked to her the day before that he was getting too stout and therefore intended to start on a course of weight reduction. He proposed to accept no more invitations to supper. She laughingly added (said Freud) that her husband, at the place where he regularly lunched, had made the acquaintance of a painter who had pressed him to be allowed to paint his portrait since he said he had never seen such expressive features. Her husband, however, had replied in his blunt manner that he was much obliged, but he was sure the painter would prefer a piece of a pretty young girl's behind to the whole of his face. The patient went on to say that she was very much in love with her husband now, and teased him a lot. She had begged him, too, not to give her any caviar.

Freud goes on to say that he asked her what that remark meant, and she explained that she had wished for a long time that she could have a caviar sandwich every morning but had begrudged the expense. Of course, her husband would have let her have it at once if she had asked him. But, on the contrary, she had asked him not to give her any caviar, so that she could go on teasing him about it.

Freud continues by asserting that this explanation struck him as unconvincing. He adds that inadequate reasons like this one usually conceal unacknowledged, and thus unconfessed, motives. They reminded him of one of Bernheim's hypnotized patients, When one of them carries out a post-hypnotic suggestion and is asked why he is acting this way, instead of saying that he has no idea, he feels compelled to invent some obviously unsatisfactory answer. The same was no doubt true of his patient and the caviar, Freud goes on to add. "I saw that she was obliged to create an unfulfilled wish for herself in her actual life, and the dream represented this renunciation as having been put into effect." But why was it that she stood in need of an unfulfilled wish?

Freud goes on to say that the associations which she had so far produced had not been sufficient to interpret the dream. He pressed her for some more. After a short pause, such as would correspond to the overcoming of a resistance, Freud said, she went on to report that the day before she had visited a woman friend of whom she confessed she felt jealous because her (the dreamer/patient's) husband was constantly singing this woman's praises. Fortunately this friend of hers is very thin, and the patient's husband admires a plumper figure. I asked her what she had talked about with her thin friend, Freud went on, and she replied, naturally, of that lady's wish to grow a little stouter. Her friend had inquired, too, "When are you going to ask us to another meal? You always feed one so well."

The meaning of the dream was now clear, Freud says, and he was able to say to his patient: "It is just as though when she made this suggestion you said to yourself: 'A likely thing! I'm to ask you to come and eat at my house so that you can get stout and attract my husband still more! I'd rather never give another supper party.' What the dream was saying to you was that you were unable to give any supper parties, and it was thus fulfilling your wish not to help your friend grow any plumper. The fact that what people eat at parties makes them stout had been brought home to you by your husband's decision not to accept any more invitations to supper in the interests of his plan to reduce his weight."

All that was now lacking was some coincidence to confirm the solution. The smoked salmon in the dream had not yet been accounted for. "How," Freud asked, "did you arrive at the salmon that came into your dream?" "Oh," she replied, "smoked salmon is my friend's favorite dish."

In the forgoing example, Freud is illustrating his central point about dreams, that is to say that they always express, in disguised form, the fulfillment of an unconscious wish. For our purposes, we can now turn directly to his exposition of the material which constitutes the content of all dreams, especially the mechanisms of disguise they can be seen to utilize. Freud saw the content of dreams as constituting a kind of rebus produced during sleep, in which the ordinary more-or-less rational logic of waking mental life is not available to the dreamer. By applying the tool of free association to the images and elements of the manifest dream (that is, what is recalled and reported by the dreamer), it became possible to unravel the defensive alterations that served to disguise the patient's underlying thoughts.

One of the primary mechanisms of distortion in dreams is the idea that a single element can stand for, or lead to, several different subjects. This Freud called "condensation," and he gives a number of examples. To briefly summarize one such dream as an illustration, Freud describes the following (in part):

"My friend R was my uncle.—I had a great feeling of affection for him. I saw before me his face, somewhat changed. It was as though it had been drawn out lengthwise. A yellow beard that surrounded it stood out especially clearly."

I shall condense Freud's description of the background, and the dream analysis, to emphasize the idea of condensation. As it turned out, R was indeed a friend of Freud's, but the connection to one of Freud's uncles, Josef, and also to another friend, N, was what determined the condensation embodied in the dream reference. The underlying subject matter which caused the linkage was the question of possible appointment to the position of professor, with which R, N, and Freud were all concerned. Uncle Josef had, years earlier, been convicted of a crime, which led Freud's father to label him a simpleton. N had been falsely accused of significant criminal activity. The yellow beard solidified the connection between R and uncle Josef, and N's accusation of criminality connected him to Josef as well. To simplify the decoding of the dream's meaning, Freud wished to assure himself that he was neither a simpleton nor a criminal, like the figures condensed in the dream material—thus, his chances of promotion should be better than theirs.

Freud's further discussion of the work on this dream led to his appreciation that the specified "great feeling of affection" was puzzling, since it did not properly relate to any of the three figures he had detected in the dream analysis. He came to conclude that this element was an example of *dissimulation,* yet another form of disguise, in this case meant to conceal the slanderous treatment of his friends that Freud had embarked upon, albeit unconsciously.

Still other mechanisms of distortion include *displacement,* a term for the shift of emphasis of a particular quality, often but not exclusively emotional, from one important element of the dream to another, apparently innocuous one, thus disguising the true underlying meaning. An example might be a dream in which a prominent public figure is humiliated, or even killed, when the underlying hidden meaning involves hostile wishes towards an important personage in the dreamer's personal life. In addition it is not unusual for the dream surface to employ complex and confusing rearrangements of time and locale, in the interest of concealing the true nature of the dreamer's thoughts and wishes.

This highly condensed description does not really do justice to Freud's elegant and elaborate presentation of the subject of dreaming and dream interpretation. Those who are interested in the specifics are urged to consult the book, which is still readily available. Suffice it to say that in any assessment of Freud's enduring legacy, his work on the interpretation of dreams must surely occupy a prominent place.

So far as Freud's lasting influence on popular culture is concerned, his ideas about dream interpretation stand alongside his famous conception of the *Oedipus Complex* as the twin pillars of his revolutionary oeuvre. As I shall try to demonstrate, these two fundamental principles are linked by more than the relative coincidence of the timing of their initial appearance. It turns out that the insight leading to his formulation of the Oedipus complex came from his application of his technique to the analysis of some of his own dreams.

During the years of Freud's relative isolation from most of the Viennese medical community, he carried on a largely epistolary relationship with Wilhelm Fleiss, a physician friend who resided in Berlin. In the course of their exchanges, he described in some detail his struggles to understand the clinical problems which he faced. The subsequent publication of some of these letters revealed that Freud employed his developing skill at dream interpretation in analyzing his own dreams. He later acknowledged that a number of the sample dreams in his great book on dreams and their interpretation were actually his own. In the course of this ongoing effort at self-analysis, Freud was very gradually able to convince himself of what was to become perhaps his most fundamental insight into sexual development.

Historians of psychoanalysis with access to his correspondence with Fleiss have identified one particular letter as crucial to comprehending Freud's discovery of the oedipal situation in his own mental life. Dated October 15, 1897, Freud wrote about the unmistakable (to him) evidence that revealed his own early childhood feelings of possessive love for his mother, and the consequent jealous and competitive feelings and thoughts about his father. Because of the resemblance of the situation to Sophocles' classic play *Oedipus Rex*, with which he, like other educated persons of his day, was familiar, Freud's self-discovery soon evoked the famous sobriquet of the "Oedipus Complex."

Until his truly momentous breakthrough of fresh insight and understanding, achieved only after what must have been a great deal of inner resistance and doubt, Freud had believed that the disturbing early sexual experiences reported to him by many of his neurotic patients were really previously buried memories of some actual events in their childhoods. These recollections invariably involved some kind of seductive treatment of them by caretakers, siblings, or even parents. The patients themselves were sure that these events had actually taken place, and told Freud about them, with difficulty, but with absolute conviction of their veracity. It is true, Freud later acknowledged, that he had begun to wonder at what seemed to be the extraordinary frequency with which such surprising, and very troublesome, events had transpired in the lives of so many of his patients. Nevertheless he apparently accepted the accuracy of these memories of trauma until his own self-analytic findings gave him reason to reconsider this data.

Eventually, as a consequence of his laborious self-analytic efforts, Freud put aside what has since been labeled the *seduction hypothesis*, which became the name for his belief that all the tales of sexual molestation in childhood actually occurred. Instead, he concluded that the "memories" of childhood seduction reported to him by so many of his patients must have been only exceptionally vivid fantasies, despite the fact that his patients apparently believed them to be memories of actual events. In time, this complex matrix of memories and fantasies earned the designation of "psychic reality" as a way of emphasizing both the patients' conviction of their veracity and of distinguishing them from actual reality.

His new comprehension of the central role played by fantasies in childhood development must surely have enabled Freud to learn about, codify and describe the apparently universal formation of a variety of sexual theories in the minds of little children. In yet another of his enduring publications, *Three Essays on Sexuality*, (1905) he outlines in fascinating detail the network of commonly encountered and early-acquired sexual beliefs that play a crucial role in the psychological development of children. It would not be practical to describe these commonly found fantasies in detail here; the interested reader can easily find a copy of this stunning monograph. A partial, abbreviated list of those phenonema most often encountered must suffice for the moment. Typical ones might involve such activities as looking and being looked at, touching and being touched, smelling, eating and a variety of excretory functions, a veritable panoply of imagined sexual acts involving the genitals, as well as the mouth and anus, more-or-less violent activities involving inflicting or experiencing pain, as well as some bizarre ideas about pregnancy and childbirth. Furthermore, Freud noticed that all children seemed to have had theories about the anatomical differences between boys and girls, and men and women. I shall have more to say about this loaded subject later on. In summary, Freud's work in this area altered forever the contemporaneous widespread cultural beliefs about the innocence and ignorance of children, and about their supposed indifference to sexual matters.

Freud plotted out a sequence of sensual foci in children, and the kinds of real and imagined activities accompanying them, which he posited would take center stage during the first six years of their lives. Perhaps even more essential to this heretofore unimagined view of childhood development was Freud's emphasis upon the immaturity of the mental capabilities of such small children. In consequence, he was certain that the rich fantasy life he was describing would inevitably be marked by confusion and misunderstanding. This entire topic became incorporated under the rubric of *infantile sexuality*, and Freud, along with many others as time went on, continued to elaborate, modify and refine those ideas and concepts for decades to come.

Before bringing this account of the initial section of Freud's career and output to a close, it is worth mentioning that during the first decade of the twentieth century, as this amazing burst of his new insights and theories was being presented to the public for the first time in his various publications, a growing group of interested cohorts and students slowly began to assemble around him. In short order, considerable turmoil also erupted, accompanied by rivalries and the emergence of definite, discrete divergences from Freud's ideas. These dynamic competitions among the members of what came to be called the "psychoanalytic movement" have been well documented elsewhere. For our principal purpose, which is to follow the progress of Freud's career and findings, it is worth pointing out that he was encouraged by some loyalists to advance a description of his particular views about proper psychoanalytic technique. This he did in a series of publications which have since become known as the *Papers on Technique* (1912-1917). The essence of that major undertaking will be presented in the next chapter, since it served to initiate the second, and significantly different, phase of his creative endeavors. Before embarking on that undertaking, however, I believe it is important to make an overriding general observation about Freud's mindset that assessors of his work do not always present clearly.

Freud's model of the neurotic disturbances he set out to study and treat was drawn from the prevailing nineteenth-century template of physical illnesses. By this I mean to say that, like infectious diseases, neuroses were assumed to be caused by some specific noxious element or condition in the otherwise presumably normal mental apparatus. Once this causative source was identified, if the doctor could successfully remove the toxin. the suffering patient might be expected to be restored to a healthy state. This was, at bottom, a biological, rather than a social, psychological conception of the emotional disorders that psychoanalysis aimed to relieve.

In contrast to this view, we now understand that both neurotic symptoms and more pervasive, often subtle character disturbances are influenced by the social and emotional matrix in which a child grows up. That is to say, in addition to his physiology, in which inherent variations in capacity and tendency always exist, each child is also indelibly impacted by his experiences with caretakers, parents, siblings, and the social environment surrounding him. This combination of factors is believed to have a determinative influence on each child's adult character structure, as well as on his proclivities to neurosis. At the present time most, if not all, mental-health professionals believe that these multiple forces and factors combine to produce the emotional and behavioral problems that psychoanalysis seeks to alleviate; but this was not part of Freud's mindset. A determined investigator could plausibly find in Freud's later work some ideas suggestive of, or contributing to, our current understanding of psychopathology, and, for that matter, of normal development as well. That said, this conceptual point of view was never his chief focus, nor was it central to his theories, within his professional lifetime.

CHAPTER III

Freud: The Middle Years: Topographic Theory and Transference

The model of the mind and its activities that Freud devised, and that he described in his writings during the second decade of the nineteenth century, has become known as the *topographical model*, since it postulates the figurative stratification of the different systems involved: the Conscious, the Unconscious, and an intermediate system, the Preconscious.. These were not to be thought of literally as actually occupying three separate spatial areas of the brain. Because of its analogy to geographical mapping, however, Freud's conceptualization led to the notion of topography as a descriptive heading for this way of dividing up the three domains of mind and thinking. He called these divisions of the mind *systems* in order to indicate that it was their respective operative characteristics that defined their differences. Thus, he underscored the idea that they were not to be assigned to different specific loci, but instead were to be understood to be functional divisions of mind. He further indicated that each of these three systems was organized by its own particular mode of activity, and suggested that there were certain definite modes of interaction among them.

The system Conscious speaks for itself; it involved and included whatever is present in the individual's awareness, either at the moment, or whenever that person's attention seeks it. Most important to understand, in Freud's view, was the essential character of the system Unconscious; all the material in it was thought to be the least conventionally organized of the three. It was conceived as being quasi-biological, inchoate, primitive, and inherently non-verbal in nature. In general, a good deal of the contents of the Unconscious system, potentially troublesome if recognized, was prevented by the forces of repression from achieving direct, clear entry into the system Conscious. On the other hand, the so-called system Preconscious was the name applied to the whole domain of thought, perception and memory that was not, at any given moment, present in consciousness. Its contents were not believed to be inherently prevented by repressive forces from being freely admitted to conscious awareness whenever the person's attention might be directed to them. In other words, the system Preconscious contained the mental material that was not believed to be the subject matter involved in intra-psychic conflicts; hence, it could be freely called forth into awareness.

According to this new, more refined model of the mind and its operations, the central psychoanalytic therapeutic task took on a different form from that previously thought crucial. It was no longer simply a matter of recognizing and then naming the traumatic unconscious thoughts and memories which were believed to be at the heart of the troublesome symptoms of neurosis. Instead of this relatively simple notion of the treatment process, therapeutic activity was now focused on identifying and somehow overcoming censorship barriers (repressive forces). These stood in silent, unsuspected, successful opposition to the emergence into conscious awareness of noxious unconscious stimuli that caused the symptoms. In effect, this revision transferred the therapeutic emphasis from simply uncovering the traumas directly to enabling their recovery by locating, identifying and overpowering the forces which blocked their emergence. Needless to add, this latter task was neither an easy one, nor was its operation simple to explain.

Freud suggested that overcoming the resistances, as the repressive forces were now called, was to be accomplished by the psychoanalyst's patient, tactful and persistent interpretation of them to the patient. This required the analyst to first recognize and identify these resistances, and then point them out to the patient, a number of times if necessary. Thereby, the patient could somehow put them aside, permitting the underlying troublesome stimuli to emerge and be recognized. This approach was certainly more complicated than the previous therapeutic technique, which was simply based on the analyst's sensitive, intuitive recognition and naming of the traumas at the root of the patient's distress.

Freud realized that this revision of the therapeutic focus entailed more work on the part of the analyst, but that it also would demand more psychological work by the patient. This new formulation of the method gave rise to the term *working through* to refer to what was required of both participants in the psychoanalytic enterprise, even though the precise nature of this work could not be spelled out. It was clear that accuracy and persistence on the part of the analyst, along with some sort of psychic effort on the part of the person who was in analysis, had to be involved in the process of "working through."

An abbreviated clinical vignette may serve to illustrate the problem of the persistence of resistance, although it does not explain this feature of psychoanalysis. A successful academic in the second year of her analysis was, from time to time, required to cancel scheduled analytic sessions in order to meet certain professional obligations. On one such occasion, although she had previously declared that she would be unable to come to her sessions on the final two days of the following week, she told her analyst that the conference she had been expected to attend had been postponed, and therefore she could, in fact come to both sessions after all. The analyst then had to tell her that one of the two sessions she had cancelled had, in fact, been assigned to another person, and thus would not be available to her after all. She was surprised, if not to say shocked, at this news, even though the system the analyst employed in respect to cancelled sessions had been explained to her at the beginning of her treatment.

During her session immediately following these events, she reported a dream in which her younger sibling appeared, to the considerable dismay of the patient, in her parents' bedroom. The analytic work on this dream introduced the theme of sibling rivalry for the first time in her analysis. Only two days later, fresh analytic material involving competitive feelings about a co-worker came forward. In the course of that session the analyst reminded her of the recent dream regarding her sibling. To the surprise of the analyst, it immediately became clear that the patient had absolutely no recollection of the dream in question, or of the analytic work on the theme of rivalry! Needless to add, many repetitive explorations of the complexities involved in her relationships with, and feelings about, rivals, became necessary before her tendency to forget or deny such issues was overcome. Working through did, indeed, necessitate both patience and work on the part of both members of the analytic twosome.

Perhaps the most important aspect of Freud's evolving theories about psychoanalysis, and the technique required in its therapeutic dimension, was his empirical discovery of the phenomenon of what came to be called *transference*. Although it had been hinted at earlier in his work, this important concept was developed much more completely and described in detail during this period of Freud's output. To Freud, the term meant simply that certain of the person's childhood wishes, perceptions and attitudes, which had originally characterized his relations to parents, siblings, and other important early figures, persist into adulthood, embedded in the unconscious layers of his mind. They were therefore potentially capable of being quite literally "transferred" on to the figure of the analyst. This process of transference was believed to take place automatically, without any specific motivation. It must be emphasized that this occurred without the patient's having any awareness of this process taking place! Thus, the transferred patterns or attitudes would be experienced by the patient as a convincingly real picture of the analyst, and of their current relationship to one another. Freud quickly realized that his recognition of transferences could provide him with a valuable tool that enabled him to see into and grasp the meaning of vital parts of the patients' unconscious minds, in particular their tendencies and attitudes within important relationships. At the same time, he could grasp something about the repressed unconscious sources of those patterns.

While the most dramatic and well publicized kind of transference is some version of a romantic and openly—or implicitly—sexual attachment to the analyst, many other forms of transference, including negative ones, also exist. It is important for the student of Freud's work in this area to keep in mind that the positive transferences, often referred to as "libidinal" ones, do not necessarily show up only as full- blown romantic or sexual feelings towards the analyst. Milder derivative versions might appear in the guise of wishes to be liked, taught, favored, or merely approved of; or, on the other hand, sensitivity to anticipated or experienced indications of the analyst's disapproval or criticism. Similarly, some varieties of negative or hostile transferences could take the form of competitive behavior or covert or open rivalry with the analyst. These can even manifest as excessive pessimism about the analysis, or noticeably stubborn refusal to accept some of the analyst's offerings and interpretations.

Incidentally, Freud later claimed that his first appreciation of the phenomena of transference was a consequence of noticing that several of his women patients became extremely admiring and enamored of him as their analyses progressed. He noted, somewhat wryly, that he became suspicious that something in their psychologies must be at work, since he had no illusion that he was in reality so attractive a man!

Once Freud had formulated the true source of these transference phenomena—as constituting a repetition or re-enactment of parts of the patient's past—he soon turned his new understanding of transference into an invaluable tool. This enabled him to see into and grasp the meaning of vitally important aspects of each patient's unconscious mind. In particular, he could better understand aspects of each patient's patterns of relationship to important persons in childhood, and perhaps also gain insight into the repressed origins of those particular elements. Freud also soon realized that transference characteristics frequently made their presence evident in various forms of action—in behavior rather than in verbalized perceptions, memories or fantasies. Thus was born the notion of a *compulsion to repeat*, a term that in time became familiar in a broader, less limited and precise sense. Originally, it was simply a reference to the idea that aspects of the transference might show up as actions which replicated crucial bits of the patient's past. Such behaviors took place without the patients' conscious recognition of either their significance or their true origins, until analytic activity was able to enlighten them.

At the same time, paradoxically, Freud came to see that the patient's transference feelings and beliefs were not merely clues to illuminating the past, but might also serve to obstruct the analysis. He came to appreciate that under certain circumstances, transference feelings and attitudes could create resistance to the analyst's efforts to bring important repressed matters forward into consciousness. The explanation of this apparent ambiguity rested in the patient's conviction that transferences were actually real perceptions, and thus they influenced the patient's feelings at every moment in the analytic session. Therefore, there were times when some transference attitudes could interfere with the patient's willingness to verbalize some of the free associations arising in his mind. These associations at times might require verbalizing some thoughts and ideas that the patient would very much prefer the analyst not to hear. Criticism, mockery or morally reprehensible notions or desires, for example, could be highly problematic to express; and thus censoring them would obviously disrupt the flow of free association.

Freud's clinical experience led him to the belief that, while difficult to execute, painstaking, patient, tactful, and gentle interpretation of the transference phenomena he recognized could, in time, convince the patient that these really originated in the past. This work would gradually make clear both the nature and origins of the patient's neurotic problems. Freud further believed that this process of enlightenment would show the patient that the unrealistic, immature ideas of childhood could now be examined, understood and re-evaluated by the patient's much more mature mind, to try to deal with mental conflicts,. These old, neurotic solutions could thus be abandoned in favor of more congenial and realistically adaptive solutions. This added up to a neat, appealing and positive clinical theory of cure in the development of Freud's still-evolving psychoanalytic experience and thinking.

As Freud continued to gain valuable clinical experience, his understanding of transference phenomena gradually increased in complexity and sophistication. In attempting to follow these changes, one must keep in mind something that is often overlooked by casual students of his work. It was Freud's unshakable belief that the clinically important transferences, both positive and negative, only take shape during the years of childhood that have become known as the "oedipal period," that is to say, roughly ages three to six, in both boys and girls. Freud called these transferences *object transferences*, meaning that they involved the mental images (thereafter called "representations") of real persons in the lives of the children, and not of inanimate things. He thought that infants and very young children, before they reached their oedipal years, were not yet mentally developed enough to be capable of attaching their wishful psychological energies (referred to as "drives") to the mental images of other people in a stable form. He imagined that during the earlier years of their development, which later became known as the "pre-oedipal" years, children were only able to invest the drive energies in parts of themselves, not in the images of other people. This opinion of his, which was later to be challenged by other thinkers, in all likelihood gave rise to the term *narcissism,* in reference to the centrality of the very young child's exclusive capacity to focus only on parts of himself, rather than on others. Despite prominent disagreements about this formulation, some emerging during Freud's own lifetime, there is, so far as I can determine, absolutely no written evidence indicating that Freud himself ever changed his mind about the developmental timing of object transferences.

Another addition to Freud's evolving ideas about transference was his proposal that, in addition to the transferences that helped to explain the sources and nature of the patient's problems, there also existed another form of transference which was to be regarded as benign, and helpful to the analytic process. Freud called this the *unobjectionable positive transference*. Since he regarded the work that the patient had to perform in analysis as difficult, and indeed often unpleasant, Freud concluded that some aspect of the patient's relationship to the analyst must help to power the analytic work, creating a positive link between them that was useful, and perhaps even essential, for the analysis to succeed. He thus differentiated this postulated form of transference from the truly romantic, erotic transferences he had discovered, which required attention and interpretation to be "resolved" in pursuit of a cure. Freud meant by the "unobjectionable" term to indicate such factors as trust, confidence—even a wish to please the analyst and gain his or her approval—that supplied motivation to help the patient overcome the resistances he had explained had to be overcome for the analysis to be successful.

This was a rather ingenious formulation, and it was not called into question for a number of years. In fact, it was in all likelihood the genesis of the belief, developed later, that the *relationship* to the analyst was actually the true vehicle of therapeutic benefit in psychoanalysis. This latter-day theory was in fact a far cry from Freud's beliefs, and it continues to be a focus of controversy in psychoanalysis to the present day. Pursuing that important topic would be a significant departure from our central task, which is to trace Freud's clinical experiences and his theoretical explanations of them, so we shall not do so here. That said, an exception must be made in order to indicate the inherent problem with Freud's formulation of the unobjectionable positive transference. His description of the milder derivative forms of libidinal transference, which had to be described and worked on for the analysis to succeed, could hardly be distinguished in their various shapes from the so-called unobjectionable ones that supposedly promoted the work of analysis! This conundrum, if not to say logical fallacy, was never remarked by Freud himself, and it was only a number of years later that his devoted followers recognized the problem, and set to one side the faulty proposal of an unobjectionable transference.

In fact, it became possible to demonstrate in clinical work that apparent elements of the so-called unobjectionable positive transference can, under some conditions, actually serve as subtly disguised forms of resistance, This, too, was long after Freud's time, and the deficiencies of his proposal were never clarified in his lifetime. It was also only later on that some Freudian theorists became aware that the phenomena of transference could be recognized as applying to persons' relationships to other figures in their lives, and not only to the analyst. Examples would include teachers, bosses, coaches, partners, colleagues, and certainly lovers and spouses. This speaks to the power of the unconscious mind to influence many aspects of an individual's life, and not merely to comprise the elements of neurosis. As important as all the later emendations of Freud's original ideas may prove, we can regard his extraordinary explorations and conceptual thinking with admiration and respect, without overlooking their imperfections and limitations.

Another very important consequence of Freud's appreciation of transference phenomena was his growing conviction that their interpretation, and analysis was actually the key ingredient that determined a positive therapeutic outcome. He seems to have decided, although he did not elaborate the thinking that led him to this conclusion, that the analysis of the transference to the analyst was, in fact, the only mechanism that had therapeutic effect. This new formulation had a profound impact on his description of the kind of psychoanalytic technique which, in his development of clinical theory, Freud recommended that all who wished to follow his example should practice.

In a series of publications from 1912 to 1917 Freud set forth his practical advice, a step that, as previously mentioned, apparently came about in response to requests from a small but growing group of his followers. In these papers he suggests very strongly that a patient's transference wishes should never be gratified by the analyst's behavior, which would certainly include both the form and content of whatever the analyst might say to the patient in the course of their work together. He explained the reasoning behind his recommendation (which would, in time to come, be challenged by the wider analytic community). He was convinced that such inadvertent or intentional gratification would be bound to render the proper analysis of those wishes much more difficult. Thus, it was not only proscribed to have romantic, much less frankly sexual, relations with any patient, but Freud also thought it important for the analyst to avoid giving any signs of love, approval, admiration, affection; to express any criticism or disapproval; or to even offer suggestions, instructions, or advice on the conduct of the patient's life.

Taking this proscription as it was intended would render perfect execution very difficult, if not to say impossible, to achieve. We are doubtless meant to take this technical standard as an ideal model, one that was not likely to be fully and precisely achieved. Instead, the aspiring Freudian analyst was encouraged to make every effort to monitor him or herself so as to avoid egregious or even intentional violations of these precepts. It is worth noting that these standards of technique are still taken seriously in many quarters; although more recent times have yielded controversy, and even sharp criticism, on the part of analysts who have elected not to follow these Freudian precepts.

Freud himself never reverted from these ideas about how to conduct a proper psychoanalysis. At one point he even noted that giving encouragement, or describing his own personal experiences as instructive examples, were at best ineffective tools, and in fact often seemed to contribute to generating patient resistance. He compared the analyst's task to that of the surgeon, with observing, listening, discovering, formulating and exploring or interpreting as the main instruments at his disposal.

One other element of Freudian theory that is worthy of further clarification is his concept of *libido*, which, as has been mentioned, is the name he applied to the energy of all of the individual's pleasure-seeking drives, including the frankly sexual ones that surface during the oedipal stage. This presumptive force was believed to be connected, during this latter period of development, to the sexual thoughts and desires that surface in the minds of all persons, rather than some quasi-hormonal substance that originated in the organs of sexuality. Nevertheless, it was conceived as having a somewhat biological quality, and thus Freud thought that this mysterious libido, when subjected to powerful repression, was in some fashion converted into a toxic product, the expression of which took the form of anxiety. Therefore, he suggested that if psychoanalytic treatment were successful, and undid the effect of the repressive forces, the libido would be "freed up," relieving the anxiety and making it possible for the patient to thenceforth enjoy more mature expressions of sexuality. A rather neat proposition—although it was soon to be discarded in favor of a significantly modified conception of the impact of treatment.

It is not hard to recognize that this theoretical construct was, at bottom, a biologically influenced picture of mental disorders and their treatment. Freud was convinced that neurotic sufferers held a fixed belief, originating in childhood, in the reality of inherent conflict between their primitive wishes and the dangerous consequences they imagined would certainly result if those wishes were detected by the adult authorities in their lives. It would in all likelihood seem to a small child that the rivalry which represented an aspect of their wishes for satisfaction (get rid of Daddy to possess Mommy, or the converse, get rid of Mommy to possess Daddy) would inevitably lead to severe punishment. Freud postulated a state of conflict between the drives—*i.e.*, wishes—and compelling ideas about the risks to self-preservation involved in their expression and detection that were designed to block, or at least disguise, them. This central notion of serious intra-psychic conflict, of which patients had no conscious understanding or even awareness, became the touchstone of Freud's conception of neurosis.

It follows logically from this schema that Freud thought that the important central conflicts in each person's mind would emerge, in some version, in their transferences to the analyst. Thus, they were very much alive and active in the so-called "present moment" of the psychoanalytic sessions. Once again, Freud's somewhat concrete biological assumptions about the nature of neurotic disturbances may be detected in his optimistic belief that the psychoanalytic uncovering and subsequent clarification, of transference could lead to cure. If we set aside the many doubts and debates about Freud's formulation of neurosis and treatment that emerged in his time and thereafter, there is still another significant red flag to which contemporary students of Freud's work ought to pay attention. By this I mean to alert the reader to the fact that the ink with which these publications were inscribed had barely had time to dry before their author clearly began to have his own doubts about them. As a result, as the next chapter will show, his theories soon began to change in fundamental ways.

CHAPTER IV

Freud: The Late Years: Structural Theory and the Rise of the Ego

To some students of Freud's long career, it is considered one of his most remarkable attributes that he had the honesty and courage to acknowledge fundamental errors in his previous thinking as he approached his 70th birthday, an age at which even the most accomplished persons are often silent and more or less content with their previous achievements. Not only did he admit those crucial errors, but he then went on to offer profoundly important revisions of his theoretical oeuvre during the early 1920's—producing some of his most significant and enduring publications, in which he set forth his final thoughts on the nature of mental processes, and the problems that psychoanalysis sought to address.

By that time, Freud had long been internationally acclaimed as the founder of psychoanalysis; he was lionized by his many devoted followers, and also attacked, and even reviled, by many others who disagreed with him, disliking and disparaging his revolutionary ideas. Nevertheless, he pursued the implications of a growing body of clinical evidence that gradually led him to the unavoidable conclusion that sweeping changes were necessary to his theories about how to think about and perform psychoanalysis.

From his writings, it is not clear to what extent he may have been influenced to make these changes by the reactions, criticisms, fresh ideas and suggestions of his friends, students and followers. Surely, it was also the case that his own growing body of direct clinical experience—his own everyday work as a psychoanalyst in practice—had, over time, also confronted him with certain limitations and errors in his earlier formulations.

One of the most dramatic of the surprising number of changes in his thinking was his abandonment of his earlier notion that repressed libido could somehow mysteriously be transformed into anxiety. This previously held idea was simply incorrect, and he soon introduced a far more complex and accurate explanation of the formation and role of anxiety in mental life. Perhaps even more significant was his new recognition that the childhood intra-psychic conflicts at the heart of neurotic disturbances were also more complicated in their structure than he had thought them to be. He learned that childhood dread of punishment—and the consequent imagined threat to self-preservation it entailed—was too simplistic an explanation to account for the conflicts connected to childhood wishes for libidinal gratification, which he had previously discovered and described.. His conception of the nature of these important conflicts had to be altered and refined.

A central feature of his revised formulations had to do with the belated recognition of the profound importance of *aggression* as a vital component of instinctual life. In Freud's thinking, aggression had now acquired the status of a fundamental drive, one that co-existed alongside the libidinal drive in its influence on mental functioning, and thus on human behavior. This change in his conception of how the mind works led him to consider afresh the complex and varied vicissitudes of both these fundamental drives, and the variety of wishes to which they gave rise. Even though Freud did not specifically describe this in his writings, it seems that his exposure to and observation of the destructive horrors of World War I must have had a huge impact on him; and it makes sense that this contributed to the new re-organization of his views on mental life.

In his written work, the first explicit clinical description of the profound psychological importance of aggression was put forth in his groundbreaking 1917 paper, "Mourning and Melancholia". His observations of severely depressed, that is to say melancholic, patients had gradually led him to propose an entirely new formulation to explain this emotional state. He suggested that the loss of an important person could stimulate a subtle, important, but totally unconscious merging of the psychic image of the lost individual with the mourner's own self-image. This postulated merging process in the mind became known as an *identification* of the person's own self with the mental image of the other, lost person. This complicated transformation made possible the direction of unconscious aggression, that is to say rage, at the lost other person (for having, in a sense, abandoned the mourner) that could be of sufficient intensity to produce the severely depressive emotional state designated as melancholia. It was also clinically evident that this melancholic state could become as deep, serious and all-consuming as to induce self-destructive, even suicidal, impulses. In a sense, murderous vengeful wishes, by means of this internal transformation, could turn against the angry individual's own self.

It was by no means easy to determine exactly what the unique psychological makeup might be that molded such susceptible persons' minds in this fashion, affecting their relationships with the lost other persons in such a way that extremely intense, dangerous mourning reactions might turn into aggressive, even murderous impulses. In fact, subsequent generations of psychoanalysts of all stripes came to question the entire theoretical proposition Freud had put forward concerning the mechanism of severe mourning reactions. In addition, the contemporary reader should also appreciate that, in Freud's time, there was as yet no science available about the chemistry of brain function and its possible effects on emotions and related mental states What is of significance regarding our study of the evolution of Freud's ideas and thinking, however, is his new formulation concerning the mechanism of melancholia. This meant that the notion he had held up to that point that *self-preservation* was a crucial, central component of intra-psychic conflicts had to be abandoned. This was so because he now envisioned self-destruction as a possibility that might sometimes overpower the inclination towards self-preservation. Freud was obliged to acknowledge instead that an overwhelming unconscious sense of guilt might at times be an important aspect of intra-psychic mental life. Aggression turned against the self, in other words, could push self-protection aside, and was capable in certain vulnerable individuals of leading to self-punitive behavior, even suicidal impulses, at times so severe as to be enacted, rather than merely contemplated.

In a difficult, highly theoretical paper which was published in 1920, "Beyond the Pleasure Principle," Freud synthesized his revised views about the importance of aggression. He now regarded it as a fundamental aspect of psychic life, alongside libido. In that essay, he also introduces the proposition that there exists in the mind the *death instinct*, a topic that came to assume quite different levels of importance and interpretation in other schools of psychoanalytic thought. Prominent among these were the interpretations and theories initiated by Melanie Klein and her followers; and, decades later, the "death instinct" took on a still different significance in French versions of psychoanalysis. On the other hand, this new concept of a death instinct came to acquire a somewhat dubious place in Freudian thought, both at the time of its introduction and even more so as time went on. For our purposes, this controversial subject can be set aside as a distraction, albeit an important one in some quarters, while we continue to pursue our central task of following Freud's own line of theoretical development. That said, the significance of aggressive instincts had by this time gained an important and permanent position in Freud's thinking, and it continued to occupy a vital place in the subsequent theoretical evolution of the Freudian school. In sum, the clinical vicissitudes of aggression now took on a degree of significance far greater than had been evident in his earlier formulations.

At least equally important to Freud's significant revisions was his gradual appreciation of the fact that the endeavor to analyze patients' resistance was not only time- consuming, but that this procedure was also a far more multifaceted and complicated task than he had originally thought. He had come to learn that repression, meaning both the process and the phenomena it produced, while it was still a central component of intra-psychic conflict, could no longer be conceived of as a single, uniform explanation of the formation of resistances. He had come to see that a variety of other mental operations linked to repression could also serve as defenses against the expression in action of undisguised drive wishes. A familiar example of this phenomenon is the automatic and quite unconscious conversion of hostile, aggressive wishes towards others into its direct opposite, an attitude of kindness and helpfulness, a defensive transformation that has become known as *reaction formation*. This process, like other types of complex defenses, takes place without the individual's having any conscious awareness of employing them—distinct from an individual who purposely and deceitfully adopts a conscious pleasant behavior in order to conceal conscious wishes to be sarcastic or critical of the person or persons being addressed.

Freud came to see that a number of other mental operations might combine with repression in complex ways to alter, block or otherwise disguise drive wishes, thus preventing their open expression. Freud designated this dimension of the mind's activities as *defenses*. Perhaps of even greater significance was his realization that these defensive operations, like the drive wishes whose expression they opposed, came into being outside of his patients' conscious awareness. In short, defenses, as well as the wishes they block, and various guilty reactions as well, might all remain inaccessible to the individual's conscious recognition, much less comprehension! No wonder then that careful, patient, repetitive and sensitive psychoanalytic work had to be employed in order to bring these components of intra-psychic conflict into patients' conscious awareness and understanding.

As a consequence of these new insights, Freud came to see that his previous topographic model of mental life was an inadequate and misleading picture of what he had come to understand about the mind's makeup and mode of operation. The important rearrangements and revisions of his theoretical characterization of mental activities were then set forth in two extremely important monographs during this third and final stage of his career. The first of these papers, which was published in 1923, was entitled "The Ego and the Id," while its companion, which appeared a few years later, in 1926, became known to English speaking readers as "Inhibitions, Symptoms and Anxiety."

In the first of these powerful publications, "The Ego and the Id," Freud set forth what has since become known as the *Structural Theory*. This new account of how the mind is organized permanently supplanted the earlier topographic model, and, in most quarters, it continues to be a foundational guidepost of Freudian thinking to this day. He proposed in this essay that the mental activities with which psychoanalysis is most concerned should be thought of as clusters of functions. Hence, the concept of structures is to be understood as metaphoric, rather than as designating portions of a concrete map of the mind. Just as topography had been an entirely figurative way of subdividing the mind, with no actual relationship to brain anatomy, these so-called structures were also invented as a linguistic and conceptual device. They, too, were not intended to constitute a description of discrete real entities, much less as physical structural elements located anywhere in the human brain.

Freud designated the newly christened *Id* as the point of origin, or locus, of the mental reflections of physical needs and their associated desires and impulses toward satisfaction—of the libidinal and/or aggressive drives and wishes. He now gathered under the newly renamed structure *Ego* the infinitely more complicated and varied set of mental functions which control and moderate the faculties of perception, thought, motility, memory and judgment. These include the capacity to evaluate external reality and to assess the qualities of the environment. Freud had previously employed this designation in a somewhat different, less precisely defined way, in his earlier accounts of psychic life. From this time on, however, the title "Ego" was meant specifically and exclusively to include the various component functions enumerated above, rather than—as subsequent non-psychoanalytic usage has come to imply—characterizing self-love or self-aggrandizement.

An essential dimension of the ego's many activities is to identify the need for, as well as to construct or employ the multiple operations of, Freud's newly elaborated roster of defenses against drive expression.

The third and final newly conceived structure, famously named the *Superego*, is meant to designate a set of functions that is associated with judgments of what is good, acceptable, desirable and safe; or, on the other hand, what might be considered bad, forbidden and dangerous. In Freud's revised developmental schema, this internal structure emerges around the close of the childhood Oedipal years, and replaces the earlier, more primitive fear of punishment at the hands of others. This last Freud had considered to be the concrete embodiment of the dangers to self-preservation that the younger child supposedly harbored. The superego thus acted as a sort of internal, independent regulator of behavior, replacing the real, or even the imagined, presence and anger of the parental authorities. Consequently, the superego also embodies various ideas about the many forms of guilt or its derivatives, such as punishment, remorse or acts of reparation, any of which may be related to the various categories of moral transgression. It also can be involved in forming good feelings about the self, if and when approved standards of thought and behavior are present.

Perhaps the loudest roll of thunder in this veritable storm of revision and refinement in which Freud was engaged during these final years had to do with his very important rethinking of the subject of *anxiety* and its role in mental life. As noted, he was obliged to drop his earlier incorrect, quasi-biological notion that anxiety was actually a toxic alteration of repressed libidinal energy. He now replaced this quaint, erroneous concept with a far more accurate understanding that anxiety is, in fact, an important and unique emotional response to the sense of danger that arises in the mind when it is faced with anything that is seen as possibly threatening harm to the self. In small children this may well come to pass whenever they are aware of instinctual wishes they believe to be forbidden, and hence dangerous. A number of such wishes typically arise during the Oedipal period of the child's development, and these would be considered quite forbidden by, and thus absolutely unacceptable to, the child's parents. In the prototypical namesake Oedipal example, for instance, a little boy could not but be convinced that his wish to get rid of his father so that he could instead possess his mother both romantically and sexually was absolutely forbidden—and, if it were to be detected, extremely dangerous as well. Further complicating this Oedipal drama for the little boy is the fact that he typically also loves and values his father, and does not want to lose him, rival though he may seem. It is certainly easy to see that this imaginary dilemma, as well as a host of other, perhaps less familiar such imaginary wishful creations Freud thought to be typical of childhood instinctual life, (to get rid of a sibling, for example) were very likely to give rise to severe, extremely uncomfortable conflicts in the child's mind. Therefore, anxiety can be understood as an altogether understandable and unavoidable reaction to the sense of danger associated with the fear of detection of these immature wishes by the child's parents, and thus of the imagined terrible consequences. Again, it is very important to remind the contemporary reader that in Freud's day, the discovery of the role of various biochemical components of brain function and their effects on various aspects of mental life (including their possible role in forming emotional reactions like anxiety) was still very far in the future. Freud's speculations and theoretical propositions, despite his foundation in biological medicine, were thus confined to what he could observe of psychological events.

To repeat, Freud had concluded that children's convictions about the forbidden nature of their various *Id*-derived wishes that sought expression led them to believe that very dangerous consequences were all too likely to follow if they were to be detected. Anxiety is thus understandable as an emotional reaction to the anticipation of this danger, whatever form it may assume. We can assume that anxiety and fear are probably more or less identical in form as experiences, but general usage would probably connect fear to actual perceptions of external danger situations, while anxiety would be the term used for imagined dangers of any nature.

Freud went on to suppose that a small amount of anxiety could be thought of as functioning mentally as a signal, which in turn could stimulate the child to activate defenses aimed at blocking off the dangerous wish altogether, or at disguising it to some degree. This is not to say that this signal anxiety is always clearly conscious, which we have no way of determining. However, it makes appealing logical sense that some such version of anxiety could serve as a warning, and therefore as an initiator of defense, rather than always appearing in full-blown form as a neurotic symptom.

If the activities that are associated with the dangerous wishes are altogether avoided, this response constitutes *inhibition*. A familiar example of inhibition might be the extreme fear of, and avoidance of, flying. Psychoanalysis typically assumes that flying therefore is unconsciously and symbolically connected to some activity that is a forbidden version of a child's wish, such as a triumph over a rival. Of course other avoidances, because of their unconscious symbolic meaning, may also occur.

While the term "inhibition" is used to describe complete avoidance of some activity, the commonly used term *phobia* is applied to the individual's conscious fear of some object or activity, and it implies a wish to avoid it, or them, if at all possible. These phobias may or may not produce complete avoidance of the activities or objects with unconscious symbolic significance, but characteristically the conscious fear of them is present in the minds of such sufferers. One of Freud's well-known published cases involved a little boy in Vienna who developed a terrified reaction to the sight of horses, unavoidable in those days. Freud's write-up of "Little Hans" (properly entitled "Analysis of a Phobia in a Five-Year-Old Boy," published in 1909) traces the complicated unconscious sources of this particular phobia, and it is readily available to the interested reader in Freud's collected papers (vol. 10, pp. 5-127).

In a parallel fashion, there might be obsessions, compulsions, and/or various physical manifestations associated with what was then known as "Hysteria," all of which were thought to be symbolically derived from some unconscious forbidden wishes, perhaps combined in some way with the defenses that may have altered their appearance. Solving the mystery of the underlying unconscious sources of these symptoms, like unraveling the thoughts and wishes that produce dreams, would require patient and sustained psychoanalytic attention. The analyst would learn to identify free associations that are triggered by the consciously recognized contents of the symptoms, or so Freud was convinced was the case.

At this point in our tracing of Freud's career and work, we shall shift our focus somewhat, and take up his ideas about the sequential steps in small children's mental development, specifically in regard to their capacity to imagine the fearful losses that might occur in their young lives if something went wrong. In order of their appearance, according to Freud's thinking, very young children could fear the actual loss of a valued person, such as either parent. Since their very immature minds were not thought to be capable of nuanced conceptions, they were supposed to dread the possible real loss of the actual individual involved, or, in more precise psychological terminology, this would be described as the loss of the *Object*, the term used to indicate the mental picture (representation) of the real person or persons in question.

The following step in the maturation of the child's mind might involve the capacity to simply imagine the threatening prospect of losing the *Love* of such important persons, rather than concretely imagining their complete disappearance from the child's world. He believed that this somewhat more subtle and complex version of a threat would be no less devastating to the little child than the earlier version of a catastrophic loss of the actual person would be.

Not much controversy seemed to have arisen about these notions of very little children's imaginary fears, but the same cannot be said about Freud's further conceptions of the threats that might take place during the next, that is to say the Oedipal period, of children's lives, roughly taking place from ages three to six. The reader will recall the description of Freud's revolutionary account of the sexual preoccupations—and the consequent set of immature fantasies and wishes that he was convinced arose to express them—during that critical formative period in the development of small children (see Chapter II for details). In terms of the sequence of dominant fears we are tracing, this Oedipal period was marked by preoccupations about castration, since the genitalia had become the focus of pleasure; and self-stimulation of one sort or another appeared to Freud to be just about universal in children of that age. Partly for this reason, this particular phase of development also became known as the *Phallic* stage, just as the preceding stages were referred to as the *Oral* stage, followed by the *Anal* stage, in obvious allusion to the parts of the child's body thought to be most sensitive and important during these respective developmental periods.

I have elected to describe Freud's now highly controversial views on this aspect of childhood sexual development here, rather than earlier in this book, because it seems that the social and intellectual climate of early twentieth-century Europe was quite different in certain respects (such as the role and status of women) from that which characterizes our present-day culture. To be sure, we are fully aware that the impact of his findings about the nature of unconscious mental life, especially of his assertions about the ubiquity of sexual concerns in the minds of very young children, was quite profound in the wider intellectual community. Indeed, in some quarters this is still true today, although the psychoanalytic world, for the most part, has accepted the general thrust of his ideas. However, the same cannot be said in regard to his assertions about some of the particulars of little boys' and girls' sexually related mental constructs. Freud's description of the typical ideas and fantasies children had about the nature of their genitalia and their functions have become central to contemporary controversies about much of the corpus of his work. Of course, students of psychoanalytic history are well aware that even some of Freud's contemporaries (Karen Horney is a noted example) objected to and differed with his ideas about female development. That said, it is surely true that the upsurge of interest in feminism in more recent times has clearly served to bring criticism of this aspect of Freud's work into more general cultural awareness. Evidence of this turn of events is not hard to come by; a vivid example of it occurred at a psychoanalytic clinical conference recently. One of the speakers, in the course of discussing a case, mentioned penis envy and castration fantasies in a woman, at which point a dozen or so young women professionals in the sizeable audience immediately rose from their seats in the auditorium and left the room!

Even in the face of this cultural shift, our present purpose is nevertheless to take up the specifics of Freud's ideas about childhood sexual development, subsequent questions aside, He asserted that the genitalia of all normal children, since they were such highly sensitive centers of pleasure whenever they might be stimulated, assumed great psychological importance to them, especially, if not exclusively, during the years of what we have called the Oedipal period of their development. He was convinced that self-stimulation of one sort or another was ubiquitous, and he further presumed it was accompanied by aspects of the rich fantasy life characteristic of the minds of children during that period of their development. He further concluded that, given the inevitable limitations of their mental capacities at that age, there must be considerable misunderstanding and confusion about the precise nature of adult sexual activities, of the nature of the act of impregnation, and the processes involved in pregnancy and childbirth.

One such example of the latter occurred in a child who thought that the mother somehow ate some kind of seed, which grew in her belly until the baby erupted through the navel like a plant!

Freud also was convinced that comparable confusion and uncertainty must be involved in the ideas children had about their genital anatomy. As for boys, the prized penis was thought to be at risk in the event of punishment for forbidden sexual wishes, which would account for the central role Freud assigned to castration anxiety in the panoply of threats that most, if not all boys imagined. As for little girls, it was Freud's theory, later to become the center of feminist controversy, that little girls could not help but misinterpret the true nature of their genitals, and upon becoming aware of the visually markedly different anatomy of boys and men, he thought they were likely to conclude that they were somehow missing the valued penis. Freud went on to guess that in such circumstances most girls would experience envy of the boys' penises, and possibly experience some combination of shame and anger at their imagined notion of deprivation or loss. Now, it is true that Freud also acknowledged in other writings of his late career that his understanding of the details of female developmental psychology was inadequate, and he went on to say that further elaboration and clarification of this area would be one of those problems that would have to be clarified by his successors! It is not clear to me how much this admission was occasioned by criticism and complaints about his thesis about little girls' development, even in his own day. There is no question at all, though, that this aspect of his theorizing has become subject to criticism, rejection, ridicule and substantial revision in more recent times. This is true, not only at the hands of outright opponents of his entire approach to psychoanalysis, but also of many thinkers who identify themselves as Freudians in their overall approach to psychoanalytic theory and practice This situation is probably familiar to most sophisticated persons interested in, and informed to some degree about, psychoanalysis in general, and Freud's work in particular. It must suffice, however, for us to recognize just what his thinking was at various times in the period we are summarizing—and that certainly ought to include some notation of its limitations.

Before we leave this question about the validity of Freud's ideas *re* the childhood confusion about the nature of female anatomy, it is necessary to take note of some reported clinical evidence that suggests that some Freudian psychoanalysts who followed his lead found his ideas useful, despite the contemporary as well as the subsequent uproar. In short, analytic work with girls and women, at least in some cases, appeared to fit well with certain aspects of his now- controversial theories. Among the most frequently reported instances, there emerged in the analyses of some women fantasies from early life of having lost their penises, for some reason or other, and a related spectrum of notions about inferiority, along with shame and anger derived from that belief. One woman, after some years in analysis, happened to recall the fantasy that, because of her childhood masturbation, her penis had somehow been turned inside out and it continued to exist inside her vagina. In another patient, the fantasy emerged that she believed that her clitoris was actually a tiny, nascent penis which would grow when she became an adult. In that woman's analysis, she also clearly remembered her confusion and resentment when she experienced her menarche, when the imagined and longed for change in her genital anatomy did not take place. While many other comparable variations of this theme have been reported, no observer could confidently assert that such reactions are characteristic of all female development. An objective observer, even today, would be obliged to acknowledge that, despite the limitations of Freud's own experience, and the debates which ensued about the accuracy of his proposals, his conception of the possible vicissitudes of little girls' misinterpretations about their bodies has a certain degree of clinical value.

To return now to tracing the progressive development of Freud's description of the various forms of conflict-related unpleasant consequences, we must take up his newly formed conception of the entity he called the "Superego," and explore the role he assigned it in regulating people's psychic lives, and thus their behavior. Freud came to believe that, as a direct consequence of the ending of the active period of the three-to-six year olds' Oedipal stages of development, each child naturally internalizes the powerful images of the parents as the judges of right and wrong, and the authors of appropriate punishment or reward. This automatic and totally unconscious process of internalization, which is also referred to as another variation of the phenomenon of "identification" (the merging of the self-image with the images of the parents extant in the child's mind), is believed to create a kind of permanent organization or structure in the child's own mind. This new intra-psychic entity, thereafter known as the superego, actually can be seen to serve as a vital step towards the child's attainment of psychological independence. From this point on, the little boy or girl no longer requires the literal presence of either parent, or activities of a regulatory nature, in order to establish behavioral modulation of the wishes, impulses and strivings that have, up to that time, depended on parental attitudes and their actual or imagined behavior.

As a direct result of this important advance in children's development, they are then believed to be capable of generating a complex network of feelings in their own minds, including, but not confined to, guilt and remorse. The child could then conceive of impulses or acts derived from these particular feelings which might be directed towards undoing the imagined sins, somehow making restitution, or embarking on some form of punishment or reparation for any real or imagined transgression. At the same time, the superego was also believed to embody imagined standards of approval or excellence, and thus was considered to function thereafter as the regulator of self-esteem. This final step completed the organization of the so-called "structural elements" that Freud now believed the internal psychic world of the child to comprise.

At this juncture we will again encounter a dimension of Freud's conception of childhood psychological development that was in time to engender criticism and controversy, as a result of his ideas about the differences between the pathways followed by boys and girls. It will be helpful to recall that the social milieu in Freud's time was substantially different from what we experience today, so perhaps his ideas about women were not as totally surprising and troublesome then as they would later prove to be.

Freud had to account for the complications that might arise from the obvious fact that children of both sexes, during the earliest years of their lives preceding the emergence of Oedipal interests and fantasies, were clearly all primarily attached to the mother images in their minds: mothers were as a rule the important caretakers of all very small children. Despite this undeniable primary attachment all children formed to their mothers, when the Oedipal stage commenced, the primary focus of love and desire for boys was unchanged; their mothers remained at the center of their loving attachment. Little girls, though, were obliged to somehow transfer their primary love interest to the image of their fathers! In Freud's thinking, it seemed logically consistent that little boys' feelings of competition and rivalry toward their fathers would lead to potent superego identification with them as dangerous punitive entities. He believed that little girls, in contrast, were not obliged to construct comparatively severe fears of their mothers, who continued to be strong objects of love and devotion. They remained the essential sustaining, nutritive figures in the little girls' lives, even when the transition to desiring their fathers as romantic and sexual ideal figures took over in their young minds. This crucially important psychological difference between girls' and boys' Oedipal situations led Freud to the dubious conclusion that the superego formation characteristic of little girls (and, to be sure, of the adult women they were to become) was inevitably less strict and punitive in nature than was true for boys' (and men's) superegos. Thus, Freud was obliged to think that the female superego was somewhat "weaker," i.e., less strict, than was the case in their male counterparts. Aside from the obvious disparagement implied by this assessment, it was simply not supported by clinical evidence, either in Freud's day or later. Therefore, this formulation of female psychological development emerged as yet another source of controversy and debate, resulting in eventual questioning of his entire picture of childhood mental life.

We now approach the conclusion of the story of the progressive evolution of Freud's own clinical observations, and the formulations and theories to which they led him. Aging and ill with an increasingly debilitating cancer of the jaw, he nevertheless continued to work and write until his death in 1939. He chose to endure the physical pain, rather than accepting narcotic medication for its relief, in order to maintain as much clarity of mind as possible.

He was still living in Vienna at the time of the Nazi *Anschluss*, as the German invasion of Austria was to be called, but after a while, through the intervention of influential friends, he was permitted to move to London, where he spent the final months of his life. Although he did write and publish other papers after the appearance of the two major monographs I have cited, some of which are still studied with interest by students of Freudian psychoanalysis, these last works do not offer substantive changes to his final theoretical constructions. The further evolution of his psychoanalytic edifice was to be left to the minds and hands of his large army of followers. These were first led by his daughter, Anna Freud, who worked closely with him during the last years of his life.

In any case, the continuing development of truly Freudian psychoanalysis was built upon the implications and central theses of his final "Structural Theory" of the mind. This stage of the growth and development of Freudian psychoanalysis was soon known by the designation, still in use to this day, of *Ego Psychology*. Its continuing story shall be outlined in the following chapter.

CHAPTER V

The Growth of Freudian Psychoanalysis After Freud's Death

What gradually became known as mainstream Freudian psychoanalysis, after the passing of its founder, turned out to be an ever-expanding network of similar, but not identical, theories and themes. Setting forth its essential shared features thus requires some selection among those features. Among the many later contributors to the growth and development of psychoanalysis, there were a number, Jacques Lacan for one, who would label themselves as "Freudians," even though they were to present ideas substantially different from anything Freud himself would ever have accepted!

In what follows, the features I have chosen to include as characterizing Freudian psychoanalysis will necessarily reflect my own preferences and point of view regarding what constitutes the essence of his legacy. I will begin by insisting on the pivotal role played by unconscious intra-psychic conflicts that originate in childhood mental life. Nothing that Freud ever wrote would challenge that this conceptual emphasis remains the centerpiece of his clinical theory. From that standpoint, Freud's later embellishments would feature ways in which crucial central drive wishes are handled, taking into account the variety of simple and complex psychological arrangements the ego devises and employs to express and disguise them. Furthermore, any such summary should include the general form of psychoanalytic treatment technique he devised, resting on the medium of free association, the use of the couch to minimize environmental distractions, and the analyst's maintaining a posture of attentive restraint. Any version of Freudian clinical technique should certainly explore and clarify the specific intricacies of the patient's mind, especially in regard to the issues with which it is preoccupied in each individual case. I also would hold to Freud's advice that the treating analyst ought to refrain from revealing much of his or her personal experience, offering directions or advice, or rendering moral judgment, praise, or even encouragement.

I shall present a condensed picture of the further growth and development of mainstream Freudian psychoanalysis, without necessarily mentioning the names of many of the esteemed thinkers and teachers who carried on this endeavor. In any such assessment of Freudian theory and its practice, however, his daughter, Anna Freud, indisputably occupies a prominent place on any compendium of those analysts who nurtured and developed the Freudian *corpus* after his death. Trained as an educator, rather than as a physician or psychologist, she was far more than her famous father's amanuensis. She was a pioneer in her own right in the development of the psychoanalysis of children; and much of her lifelong creative activity was devoted to exploring and describing the steps in the psychological development of individuals from early childhood to adulthood. She is probably best known for her authorship of the monograph *The Ego and the Mechanisms of Defense*, which was first published in German in 1935, and in all likelihood was written with some measure of input from her aging father. This work was destined to become one of the fundamental building blocks of the then emerging theoretical schema known as *Ego Psychology*.

The primary purpose of this summary of Freud's work, and of his enduring contributions to psychoanalytic knowledge and practice, is to highlight what he himself discovered and emphasized.

Accordingly, my brief and condensed account of the subsequent evolution of what we call Freudian psychoanalysis will only highlight a few major trends which were not yet in evidence during his lifetime. I shall concentrate our attention upon three major topics;

1) *Pre-oedipal* developmental theory and the clinical consequences thereof.

2) The emergence of and subsequent emphasis on *Counter-transference* as a useful tool in the technique of psychoanalytic practice.

3) The shift in the intellectual *zeitgeist* away from reliance on what had always been assumed to be the reliability of an expert analyst's objective judgment—and the related authoritative interpretation of reality and meaning as dependable tools in the analyst-observer's practice of psychoanalytic therapy. This latter posture was to be challenged, and eventually replaced, during the last part of the twentieth century by the new, nearly revolutionary, emphasis on what came to be called *Subjectivity,* or *Relativism.* These were the determining factors to influence the interpretation of the clinical situation, and consequently, the theory and practice of psychoanalysis.

Although Sigmund Freud did name and describe the earliest childhood developmental stages, he was not inclined to attribute to them important independent clinical derivatives. As mentioned previously, the oral stage came first in childhood life, consistent with the infant's primary preoccupation with feeding; and this was followed temporally by the so-called anal stage, in recognition of the developmentally appropriate focus on the slightly older child's efforts to establish conscious control of his bowel (and bladder) functions. Since Freud always believed that genuine emotional investment in the mental representations of other people only became possible when children grew somewhat older, around age three, his ideas about clinically important issues were centered on the Oedipal period and the psychological complexities which arose during those years.

It is true that one of Freud's most important and influential contemporaries, Karl Abraham, not only focused attention on the pre-oedipal stages of life and development, but also suggested that there might be certain clinical syndromes connected to them. Even more significant were the contributions of Anna Freud, as well as those of her contemporary and rival, Melanie Klein (of whom more later) to the study and treatment of small children— thus facilitating closer investigation of the details of the pre-oedipal years.

Thereafter, a certain segment of what might be considered the "Freudian analytic school" commenced to take careful note of and describe specific conflicts which they believed might arise during the oral and anal periods of children's development. In the interest of brevity, I shall not attempt to cite the many individual contributors to this growing portion of the spectrum of clinical theories, nor to describe any of the clinical syndromes that various analysts proposed might be derived from those early conflicts. Suffice it to say that some Freudian analysts were to place more emphasis on the problems they thought to be associated with the oral and anal stages of development—and their possible manifestations in clinical work with adults, as well as with children—than did many of their Freudian colleagues. That said, it is certain that all Freudian analysts retained a conviction that a variety of conflicts arising during the Oedipal years would influence subsequent development, both normal and pathological in nature, in crucial ways. They continued to think of those sets of conflicts, and their quite varied consequences, as important issues that regularly appeared in their clinical practice.

As an important aside, it is worth noting that the worsening socio-political environment in continental Europe during the decade of the 1930's led many psychoanalysts of the Freudian and other schools (not only those who were Jewish, of whom there were many, but also those who were politically liberal as well) to emigrate. Their subsequent influence on the mental health profession in England, and in both North and South America,

grew in proportion to their expanding numbers. This development was still further enlarged and enhanced by their subsequent
participation in the medical services of the armed forces during
World War II. As a result of this contact, psychiatric education
during the immediate post-war years, especially in the United
States, incorporated the powerful impact of psychoanalytic
thinking. This was so because other medical colleagues, and
especially psychiatrists, had, up until to that time been generally
unaware of current psychoanalytic precepts and practice. As a
result of this change, not only did psychoanalytic training expand
greatly, but derivative versions of psychodynamic therapies sprang
up and soon came to dominate the field. It will help the reader to
understand this shift in emphasis if one keeps in mind that
effective pharmacological treatments for various forms of mental
illness only began to appear during the latter part of the 1950's.
Thus, the explosive importance of drug treatment of all sorts only
came on the medical scene during the last part of the twentieth
century.

To return to our current topic, the trends that appeared in the
Freudian tradition after the founder's death, we shall now consider
the very important subject of the emergence of, and subsequent
emphasis on, the utilization of the psychoanalyst's counter-
transference reactions as a useful tool in psychoanalytic treatment.
The term *counter-transference* came to mean the totality of the
treating analyst's internal emotional and ideational responses that
transpired while he or she was engaged in psychoanalytic work
with the patient.

This important addendum to the treatment armamentarium
was first introduced by certain of the immediate devotees of
Melanie Klein's substantially different (from Freud's) theories and
proposals about both the psychological development of children
and the pathological conditions that might emerge from them, as
well as the alterations to treatment protocols that she also introduced. Articles published in the 1950's presented the idea that the
analyst's emotions and thinking could be influenced directly by

emanations from the patient's psyche. This notion went far beyond Freud's early metaphor which had suggested that the analyst's mind functioned like a telephone receiver that could collect and consciously interpret what the patient was saying. Instead, this new idea proposed that the patient's mind, utterances and behavior would have a direct influence on the mind of the analyst—immediate, automatic and at first unconscious—manifesting itself as what became known as his or her counter-transference: the analyst's own inner thoughts and emotions. It followed from this thesis that the analyst, by paying conscious attention to what was going on in his or her own mind, would be learning something precise about what was going on in the mind of the patient at that moment. Making use of this data was an essential device that should affect the analyst's technique.

For some years thereafter, most Freudian analysts argued vehemently against the validity of seeing this as reliable data about the patient's mind, and thus rejected the utilization of this conceptual and technical innovation. Freud himself had barely mentioned the subject of counter-transference, and had regarded it as a potential obstacle to proper understanding of the patient's psychology. He thought it referred to unconscious aspects of the analyst's own mental processes which could interfere with accurate responsiveness, rather than aiding the analyst to clarify and enlighten what the patient was saying and doing, . His views strongly influenced the decade or so of debate about this topic. In the course of time, however, the term "counter-transference," and the broad concept to which it referred, gained widespread acceptance throughout the psychoanalytic profession, many Freudian analysts included.

Rather than further describing or elaborating the subject of counter-transference, and its growing employment in the thinking and work of many practitioners, we might think of its ascendance as a signal that the prevailing epistemology of the psychoanalytic world, as well as that of the wider intellectual climate in Europe and the Americas, was about to undergo a profound shift in tone.

In Freud's day, and for some decades thereafter, the psycho-analyst, like many expert observers in other fields, could rely on the unspoken, but by and large unquestioned, belief that he or she was a reliable, essentially objective authority on what was true in the arena that was being examined. In the case of the psychoana-lyst's work, that meant the interpretation of meanings hidden or revealed in the patient's utterances and behavior. By extension, it also applied to the analyst's ability to assess what was realistic in terms of evaluating the world around patient and analyst alike. For a host of reasons that are beyond the scope of this inquiry, the prevailing conception of the reliability of all authorities, especially in science, began to change dramatically during the latter years of the twentieth century.

Seminal psychoanalytic papers published as early as 1969, by Jacob Arlow, a highly respected mainstream Freudian analyst, teacher and thinker, provided a compellingly convincing explana-tion of exactly why this comfortable assumption about any person's ability to make such objective and reliable assessments was deceptive. He proposed that one's perceptual screen showing what was occurring in the outer world was always simultaneously being more or less influenced by a stream of unconscious think-ing. This might alter the accuracy of perception, thought and judgment, all without the individual having any conscious recog-nition of what was happening. He described careful, solid clinical work which had led him to this unsettling conclusion.

It was hardly news that there were *some* individuals who *some* of the time arrived at manifestly illogical and unreasonable judgments and decisions. It was also generally assumed that such events reflected the influence of some unknown psychological, social, or political forces operating in the minds of persons so affected. Arlow's synthesis and conclusions were disturbing and even revolutionary because of his clear implication that every single person could be vulnerable to such unconsciously derived distorting forces, at any time.

The emotional difficulty in accepting this implicit challenge to having absolute confidence in one's own mental objectivity and reliable rationality was, and still is, enormous. Arlow himself, despite his clear-cut observations, and the uncompromising conclusions that he drew from them, never, even after his publications on the subject appeared in print, seemed to have applied this cautionary warning to his own habitually confident, authoritarian, psychoanalytic posture! Most others in the community of psychoanalysts were reluctant to absorb and accept this disturbing, troublesome new perspective. The same stubborn resistance to accepting the applicability of this upsetting insight into the limitations of human objectivity, judgment, and rationality also applied to the broader intellectual world outside of the relatively small psychoanalytic quorum. A moment's reflection should suffice to underline the common human tendency to maintain the unspoken but potent belief that some of us are immune to this failure of rational capacity, at least some, if not all, of the time.

Despite this all too human understandable reluctance, it is evident that very gradually the prevailing belief in objectivity, reliable reason, and positivist authority, gave way to a fundamentally relativistic or subjective outlook across the psychoanalytic spectrum. In retrospect, one might take note that the latter years of the twentieth century witnessed a cultural shift, at least in the West, which popularized the questioning of authority in politics, religion, cultural mores, and even science. In light of this powerful widespread intellectual upheaval, it is ironic that Freud and Freudianism, which originated as a radical movement at the beginning of the 20th century, became somehow transformed into the exemplar of orthodoxy, conservatism and authority!

CHAPTER VI

Freud's Enduring Legacy

This has been a brief summary of Sigmund Freud's observations, imaginative speculations, and theoretical conclusions, as they developed and changed in the course of his ongoing attempts to understand and treat emotional illnesses. It now seems fitting to try to select from the corpus of his work certain features which have endured as aspects of our contemporary view of mental life and its effects, not only on illness and treatment, but on our culture. To be sure, any such compilation as the one I shall essay to provide will surely reflect personal preferences, if not to say biases. Others would doubtless differ with the choices I offer, and still others would choose to minimize or discount such an enterprise altogether. It is certainly the case that Freud and his discoveries were in his time, and in the present day as well, nothing if not controversial. Profoundly disturbing to many in the psychological community, they were and are at least equally so to the broader intellectual community. Nevertheless, I consider it a fitting epilogue to the story of his career in psychoanalysis to suggest a summary of certain ideas that, in my view at least, have proved to be timeless and enduring.

Fundamental to any distillation of Freud's unique creativity and its lasting consequences is his exploration of the nature and significance of the unconscious portion of the human mind. His focus was not on the automatic functioning of the brain's capacity to register and interpret sights, odors and sounds, or to initiate body movements or experience certain emotional reactions, all of which occur without any conscious effort. Instead, his interest was aimed exclusively at identifying the precise contents of the unconscious mind and discovering their effects on mood and behavior, and to exploring and understanding the processes that govern those contents. Therefore, central to our examination of his special contribution will be his attention to, and subsequent explication of, the particular patterns, predilections and tendencies of each person. The motivations for these lie undetected (and usually unsuspected as well) in the depths of people's minds. In that endeavor he was unique, and he traversed territory that was never before explored in the fashion that marked his research.

As a point of departure, let us consider the well-known fact that any group of individuals exposed to the same environmental stimuli will be very likely to interpret them somewhat differently from one another, and are also quite likely to remember and recount them accordingly. A striking example of this tendency was brought to my notice not long ago in the course of a discussion I had with a distinguished professor of history. He described the broad differences to be found in the memories of soldiers and observers of a famous Civil War battle. This was true not only of contemporary reports and letters, but was even more strikingly evident in memoirs penned some time after the events in question. Historians are likely to search for socio-political factors which might have played a role in determining such differences— more or less conscious personal biases that could contribute to such differing memories and evaluations.

Freud, however, was precisely interested in identifying and comprehending those purely psychological determining features of people's minds, silent and removed from the individuals' conscious awareness, but nevertheless influencing, to a greater or lesser degree, each person's judgments, actions, emotions and convictions, and memories. In short, he wished to study and understand how these unconscious psychological features acted on and helped to shape all aspects of motivated human behavior.

As we know, he initially set out on this journey of exploration in order to clarify, and, he hoped, correct pathological responses and behaviors; in other words, to better treat the symptoms of emotional disorders. In the fullness of time, Freud's followers were to extend this process of exploration and explanation into the broader realm of looking at so-called "normal" mental activities as well. To facilitate this review of his legacy, I shall now very briefly summarize the main points of what I have recounted in greater detail in previous chapters.

Very early in his investigation of psychopathology, and the precise nature of its unconscious determinants, he uncovered the central role played by sexual wishes and fantasies, in memories of actual or imagined disturbing experiences, and in concerns for self-preservation in the face of real or anticipated threats. As he gained more experience, he came to add aggressive and self-punitive elements to his catalogue of unconscious motivating factors. In time he was also able to develop and describe a more complete and explicit version of his list of real and imagined threats; he specified their origin in the immature minds of little children, and documented their undetected persistence in the unconscious stratum of his adult patients' minds. He also learned to pay attention to the attitudes and devices that were rooted in the unconscious minds of people by means of which troublesome wishes (and fears associated with them) might be disguised. Alternately, they could be otherwise deflected into producing other, presumably safer, modes of satisfaction. And finally, it was also important that he focused his attention on how internally conceived threats could be executed, altered, and even avoided altogether, while still appreciating that all of these important mental operations could take place outside of a person's conscious awareness.

Once again, it fell to those who followed him to pursue the further elaboration of this set of important mental processes. Some of those who differed with him, in his time and afterwards, were inclined to delete or modify his troublesome ideas, or substitute new versions of the motivational components and qualities of the unconscious mind. That said, it is literally impossible to overlook, discount or minimize Freud's incredibly important role in the exploration and mapping of the "Terra Incognita" of the unconscious layer of the human mind. He was the first and most thorough demonstrator of its profound, significant role in influencing our perceptions, moods, actions, memories and judgments; in short, all of our psychologically influenced behavior. If that had been all that he achieved, it would still be sufficient to ensure him a place in history. But his legacy extends well beyond that single momentous accomplishment.

The emergence of this new perspective on the nature of mankind's mental processes was soon to give rise to speculations about how much people's unconscious minds might play a role in determining how we all understand history literature, art, mythology, and even our belief systems. While not everyone climbed aboard this bandwagon, it is easy to imagine that Freud and certain of his followers, students and other contemporaries might have easily become convinced that they were in possession of a special kind of code book. In using it they were empowered to bring fresh and original insight into the construction and hidden nature of all sorts of products of the mind.

In fact, for a significant number of analytically sophisticated thinkers, even to this day, there is a tendency to employ the application of their special expertise in the "analysis" of notable persons whom they have never actually met, as well as to their productions, be they works of literature, pieces of art, or even socio-political attitudes and activities. This fascination frequently leads to publications expounding such explanations. Some such essays are loaded with carefully assembled supporting details, while there are many others that are less comprehensively scholarly in design. In any case, they are likely to offer speculative conclusions, frank guesses, or similar interpretive expositions describing the possible unconscious determinants in the lives and works of their subjects.

There is no doubt that there are many scholars who might re-gard this plethora of publications as a living testament to Freud's enduring influence. At the same time, there are also many others who are less inclined to embrace this outpouring with enthusiasm, since they are more or less skeptical about attempting to apply psychological awareness to a person whom they have not directly examined. The latter individuals think of these efforts as a purely speculative hobby, albeit a rather popular one. Well-known examples of psychoanalytic interpretations of works of art include a work by Ernest Jones, an important British contemporary of Freud, whose monograph on Hamlet and Oedipus achieved considerable and enduring popularity, familiar in its overall concept even to many who have not actually read it in its entirety. Even Freud himself pursued such an exploration in detail in his paper, "Leonardo Da Vinci and a Memory of his Childhood" (1910). This is highly imaginative in nature, and it is also worth noting that Freud includes, late in this essay, a brief note to the effect that any such project was inevitably subject to the limita-tions inherent in the amount and quality of the available material about the subject. At any rate, it is certainly the case that one still encounters the characterization of such interesting but speculative undertakings as "Freudian" in nature.

On the other hand, there is another class of phenomena that is clearly and permanently emblazoned with the label "Freudian," which consists of commonplace errors such as forgetting, mis-naming, and other slips of the tongue, as well as analogous mistaken expressions and actions that contradict their apparent intended meaning. During the early years of Freud's discoveries about the unconscious mind's effects, he made a number of observations about a host of surface activities that were often affected by hidden psychological influences. He published a compilation of such happenings that he entitled *The Psycho-pathology of Everyday Life*(1901). To this day, it is not unusual for people hearing another person's utterance in which the clearly intended meaning has been inadvertently altered or contradicted to dub such incidents as "Freudian slips." In the hands of the mildly sophisticated observer, such an attribution is likely to take place only when the "true" underlying meaning of the slip is readily apparent; the person who commits the blunder is, as a rule, for the moment at least, unaware of its having occurred or of its significance.

The many examples of such slips that are cited by Freud in his book on the subject are, for the most part, less than clear to English-speaking audiences, since they usually involve instances in which a familiarity with the German language would be required in order to understand the plays on words, inadvertent substitutions and the like, that they employ. In order to demonstrate the point of his compilation of errors of this sort, however, I will quote one such example which can be readily grasped, even in English translation. Freud describes an instance mentioned to him by one of his contemporaries, in which the latter wrote, "You probably still recall the way in which the President of the Lower House of the Austrian Parliament opened the sitting a short while ago; 'Gentlemen I take notice that a full quorum of members is present and herewith declare the sitting *Closed*.'" The gentleman reporting this example went on to suggest that the official involved evidently expected little good from the assemblage, and secretly wished for it to be over!

To move on further in our summary, one can readily appreciate that the innovative technical method Freud devised for conducting his psychological investigations is inextricably connected to their outcome, as well as to other subsequent achievements. You will recall that after Freud gave up using hypnosis as an investigative tool, he changed to urging his patients to speak freely about whatever thoughts were passing through their minds. After at first trying to direct the patients' focus to thoughts connected with their symptoms, he soon discovered that simply urging them to adopt a completely open, uncensored and unrestricted mode of expression paid greater dividends. Meanwhile he as analyst adopted an equally open and unrestricted mode of listening to them This technique that Freud devised and employed soon became known by the designation *Free Association*, and it became a fundamental technical tool various versions of which continue to occupy a central place in most "talking treatments" to this day. In fact there are even some psychoanalysts of whatever conviction who would hold that Freud's innovative methodology, rather than his observations and theories, is the single most important and valuable aspect of his legacy to the profession.

Exactly how Freud came up with his revolutionary new technique is not entirely clear from his writings, but it should be kept in mind that Freud was convinced from the start that free associations would inevitably be influenced by the current unconscious mental activities of the individual involved. Consequently, he believed that whatever was verbalized, and also whatever might cause abrupt shifts of subject—pauses, hesitations, and the like— would serve to discern, identify and uncover unconscious thoughts and impulses. He thus assumed that, by employing this technique, he could gain access to traumatic buried memories, and, later on to thoughts and fantasies of an important, generally conflict-laden nature. Thus, this original technical breakthrough developed into the cornerstone tool for Freud's exploration of the unconscious mind.

We need not go further here in outlining Freud's methodology, the refinements developed by his successors, or the changes initiated by later rivals. It would be moot, however, to further elucidate the challenges and potential complications attendant on assuming the mental stance Freud had prescribed to be adopted by any psychoanalyst utilizing his recommended technique. As noted, he had become convinced that the analyst, rather than focusing on symptoms or any other specific subject, ought to strive to maintain a posture of receptive freedom, a tactic that came to be known as *evenly hovering attention*. In a well-known analogy, Freud likened this proposed stance to the analyst's functioning as the equivalent of a telephone receiver attuned to all of the patient's communications. He added that this posture should be employed with a degree of freedom similar to that which he had advised patients to strive to achieve. In other words, he thought the analyst should listen with unplanned and spontaneous sensibility to the emanations from the couch.

Freud himself never explicitly altered this recommendation, but in years to come, although some analysts did continue to employ this model, there were a number of others who came to think that it was neither possible nor even advantageous to do so. It is nevertheless important to remember that Freud's advice about this technique was formulated at a very early stage in his work, when his chief interest was in trying to detect the buried noxious contents that resided unrecognized and hidden in his patients' unconscious minds. As his interests evolved in later years, he came to focus more on identifying all the elements of unconscious conflicts—wishes, defenses, punishment fears and reactions—and their multifarious combinations. This was a more complex task, to be sure, than what he had thought was needed at the beginning of his work. Because of this change, some came to think (never Freud himself) that uninhibited, task-free listening might be better accompanied, at least at certain times, by some degree of focused reflection.

Although Freud himself did not ever devote much time or energy to correcting in detail his opinions or recommendations about technique, some of his successors, notably his daughter, Anna Freud, did indeed do so. Without explicitly setting aside the notion of "evenly hovering attention," she did reformulate, or rather clarify, what she considered to be the analyst's ideal position in regard to the patient's communications. She advocated that the analyst should adopt a posture of total *neutrality,* by which she meant that the analyst ought to be equally interested in uncovering and understanding all of the aspects of the unconscious conflicts burdening each patient. She believed and taught that this could best be done if the analyst took great care not to seem (much less to behave or indicate in any way) to be in favor of any of the ideas expressed. In other words, the analyst should be seen as neither condoning nor condemning, encouraging or discouraging, urging or forbidding the wishes uncovered, nor adopting any stance in respect to their potential consequences. No easy matter, to be sure; but this formula, which was adopted by many of the Freudian "ego psychologists" who followed her lead, emphasized that the analyst should not be morally judgmental or educational (except about the contents of the patient's unconscious mind); neither should the analyst be involved in advising or subtly directing or urging his patients in respect to real-life decisions and activities.

A moment's reflection should suffice to appreciate that in order to maintain such a "neutral" posture, and the recommended comprehensive unbiased receptive sensitivity, the analyst must make every effort possible to be in touch with his or her own emotional inclinations, blind spots, special interests, and prejudices. An extensive personal psychoanalysis to identify and clarify such factors, if not to altogether eliminate them, is an absolute requirement for all those training to become psychoanalysts. It would be naïve, however, for anyone to suppose that the ability to maintain the sort of perfect, undistorted self-sensitivity described above is really possible. The analyst is simply enjoined to do the best that he or she can in this respect, and also to exercise all possible care to detect and modulate the occasional inevitable lapse that may occur.

The entire network of the analyst's personal reactions and responses came in time (long after Freud's death) to be known as "counter-transferences"; however, Freud himself barely made mention of such potential interferences with accurate, helpful receptivity. It remained for later generations of practitioners to look at and study in detail this aspect of conducting psychoanalytic treatment. In consequence, important and even prominent as this topic is for contemporary psychoanalysts, it is not properly to be considered an aspect of Freud's legacy.

Of all the dimensions of mental life that Freud's methodology came to illuminate, that of the interpretation of dreams is probably the one most often associated with his name to this day. Of course, the idea that the hidden meaning of dreams could be detected, especially by those individuals who were gifted with special powers of interpretation, long antedated Freud and his work. Seers, shamans, fortune tellers, even the Biblical Joseph, among many such prophets, were thought to be able to find clues to the future in the dreams of others, or of themselves. Freud's quest was of an altogether different nature. He came to believe that decoding dream imagery offered a pathway to uncovering certain unconscious wishes, fears, memories, and thoughts that occupied peoples' minds. It became his conviction that while someone is asleep, and therefore in the mental state during which dreams take place, the mind's means of disguising troublesome ideas and wishes must be less complete, intact and powerful than while he is awake. Freud was thus convinced that access to the important and pertinent unconscious material, whether in the form of wishes, memories, ideas, or fears and fantasies of all sorts, ought to be possible with the use of proper methodology. Having worked out his ideas and technique, he published his famous book on the subject, *The Interpretation of Dreams* in 1900, more than a century ago, amending the original version somewhat over the course of succeeding years.

Freud conceived of the imagery of dreams as constituting a sort of rebus or puzzle, and he described certain elements and varying forms of disguise that characterize their peculiar formation. In time, he also speculated about the different varieties of mental activity that might be in effect in the unconscious stratum of people's minds. Our present task, however, is to suggest what might be considered his lasting legacy, so it will suffice to say that he applied his free-association technique to the task of decoding the hidden meanings of the reported dreams his patients provided (as well as some of his own dreams). I believe it is not an exaggeration to assert that Freud's work on the interpretation of dreams constituted a breakthrough sufficiently original and important to assure him a prominent niche in the history of science—even had he done nothing else of such significance in his lifetime.

Freud demonstrated that unraveling the imagery of a patient's dream permitted the analyst to have a better look at the dreamer's underlying mental preoccupations on the night in question. His approach allowed him to uncover connections and draw inferences from what the patient described about concerns that were troublesome at the time. As with other aspects of Freud's legacy, addenda, emendations and challenges to his views on dream interpretation have emerged in the decades since his death. All the same, it seems fair to say that Freud's work on the interpretation of dreams, in relatively unaltered form, remains in the armamentarium of many contemporary practitioners of psychoanalysis.

If there is one other feature of Freud's groundbreaking findings and assertions that might rival his work on dream interpretation, it is his revolutionary revision of the understanding of the psychological development of small children. Departing from the prevailing notion of childhood innocence, he discovered and emphasized instead that children had an ubiquitous interest in, as well as theories and fantasies about, sexual activities, pregnancy and childbirth, and genital anatomy, although much of this was subject to repression as children grew older.

His work in this area, according to his own account, was originally derived, much to his own surprise (as he claimed in later writings), from his investigation of the causes of neurotic afflictions. His confident overthrow of the previously held mythical belief in the ignorance and indifference of little children about sexuality has remained a pillar of his *oeuvre*. Especially disturbing, and generally unwelcome, was his outlining of the idea that little children are very interested in the sexual activities of their parents, giving rise to a set of propositions that is commonly, if incompletely, collected under the rubric of the Oedipus Complex. In any case, there can be no doubt that Freud's co-opting of the name of Sophocles' central character in *Oedipus Rex* continues as perhaps the single most well-known and enduring feature of his legacy.

Another one of Freud's most significant and original contributions to psychoanalysis, and to the study of the way the mind functions, was his discovery and explication of the phenomenon he termed "transference." It is interesting that this enduring element of talking therapies of all sorts, unlike other familiar aspects of his work, is not as a rule associated with his name. It is a fact that he was the one who first observed its presence, conceptualized its true nature, and employed it as a vital element in his mature versions of the practice of psychoanalytic therapy. Many of Freud's successors have certainly elaborated and emended this feature of mental life, but nevertheless this concept remains an important clinical conception to this day. The identification of the phenomenon of transference stands as a true monument to his powers of observation, and to his ability to organize and explain his findings.

Freud's ideas about transference became clear to him as he realized that his analytic patients regularly began to express ideas and attitudes about him that were not at all consistent with his actual *persona*, nor of his behavior towards them. His comprehension of this discovery came to fruition when he realized that the distortions he observed were actually characteristic of his patients' thoughts, wishes, fears, reactions, and relationships with important persons in their respective childhoods—usually, but not exclusively, parents. Therefore, he named this mental tendency "transference" in order to indicate that this aspect of the mind's activity was literally something transferred from past relationships onto the figure of the analyst in the present setting.

We have seen how Freud made ingenious use of his discovery of the transference phenomenon in his evolving psychoanalytic technique. He began to systematically describe to his patients what he had noticed, as tactfully and patiently as he could. In time, this procedure led to clear identification of the original sources of these transferred expressions. In due course, he learned to treat the identification and interpretation of the transference as a key element in his treatment method, and soon came to believe that this aspect of the work was the sole reliable lever that could bring about real changes in his analytic patients. He never quite explained how he arrived at this conviction, but there are to this day segments of the psychoanalytic community that cling to this belief about the mechanism of treatment. There are also others who have come to disagree with this idea—not that they dismiss the interpretation of transference from their therapeutic arsenal— but they do not think that this aspect is the only mechanism leading to positive therapeutic action in the clinical setting. Setting the controversy just described aside, it is undoubtedly true that the systematic examination and interpretation of the transference in psychoanalysis (and in many forms of psychoanalytically based psychotherapies) continues to be a defining feature in therapy across a wide spectrum of "talking treatments" to this day.

Before we leave the subject of transference, it is important to make note once again of the fact that there is a broad spectrum of transference reactions and manifestations, not only the classic romantic-love versions that are familiar to most casually informed persons. It is true that so-called erotic transferences were the first ones studied and described by Freud, but frankly sexual ones are probably outnumbered by derivative versions, such as undue admiration of the analyst, seeking favorable attention from the analyst, and other such milder expressions of libidinal transference. Freud and others also soon became aware of the existence of a host of other, so-called negative transferences. These were rarely overtly hostile, but took such forms as subtle defiance and/or rejecting and competitive behavior, any one of which might profoundly affect the course of the treatment, perhaps even permanently. One notable case with which I am familiar involved a bright young person whose father, an enthusiast of psychoanalysis, had pressured the youngster into undergoing analysis. Although this young patient was seemingly agreeable and cooperative during sessions, the treatment went nowhere for several months. When the analyst acknowledged the impasse, the young patient's reaction was not disappointment, but rather visible relief, if not pleasure! Subsequently, the young patient admitted having problems, and asked the same analyst if there were some other way to try to be helpful. A bit taken aback, the analyst suggested they might try psychotherapy in which less frequent sessions, conducted *vis-à-vis*, rather than using the couch, would be the approach. In short order, the young patient showed marked improvement, and somewhat later on, wryly admitted being very resentful about being "forced" into analysis. No longer needing to be covertly defiant, the patient was able to utilize the analyst's help quite well.

One further note about transference phenomena and their consequences is worth calling to the reader's attention. In time, it became evident to sophisticated observers that transference reactions were not confined to the analytic setting alone. Other important individuals in any person's life, like teachers, coaches, bosses, lovers and spouses, even political or religious leaders, are all potentially subject to being invested with what are actually transference influences from the subject's past. Not everyone who might be aware of this situation realizes that its discovery and identification are justly to be attributed to the work of Sigmund Freud.

I will conclude my account of the enduring features of Freud's many findings and theories by re-emphasizing his truly revolutionary investigation, and subsequent description of, the profound importance of unconscious intra-psychic conflicts and their consequences, as essential to comprehending much of human behavior. As time went on, this unsettling formulation was subject to further refinement, and also, in some quarters, vigorous dispute. Freud's opinion on this subject, however, unlike other aspects of his theorizing, never changed; unconscious conflicts of various kinds remained at the very crux of his understanding of psychic pathology. A case could be made that the impact of this perspective on people's development was, remains, as troublesome and controversial as any other component of Freud's legacy. Expert controversy aside, it rests in the hands of the educated observer to decide what proposition on this subject is the most persuasive. If one were inclined to allow Freud himself a final word about his legacy, it might be something like the following: "In years to come, they will remember that I said that dreams have meaning, and children have sexual lives, and both those things were very well known to every nursemaid in Vienna."

References

Abraham, K (1921). Contributions to the Theory of the Anal Character. In: Stein, D.J, Stone, M. H. (Ed), *Essential papers on Obsessive-Compulsive Disorders.* New York: New York University Press, 1997.

——. (1924a). The Influence of Oral Eroticism on Character-Formation. In: Perzow, S. M., Kets de Vries, M.F.R. (Ed) *Handbook of Character Studies: Psychoanalytic Explorations.* Madison, CT: International Universities Press,1991.

——. (1924b). A Short Study of the Development of the Libido. In: Frankiel, R.V. (Ed) *Essential Papers on Object Loss*, New York: New York University Press, 1994.

Arlow, J.A. (1969). Fantasy, Memory, and Reality Testing. *Psychoanalytic Quarterly* 38:28-51.

Freud, A. (1935). *The Ego and the Mechanisms of Defense.* London: Hogarth Press.

Freud, S. (1909). Notes Upon a Case of Obsessional Neurosis. In: Two Case Histories ('Little Hans' and the 'Rat Man'), *Standard Edition* X: 151-318.

——. (1910). Leonardo Da Vinci and a Memory of his Childhood. In: Five Lectures on Psycho-Analysis, Leonardo da Vinci and Other Works. *Standard Edition* XI: 57-138

——. (1900). The Interpretation of Dreams. *Standard Edition* IV: ix-627.

——. (1909). Analysis of a Phobia in a Five-Year-Old Boy. In: Two Case Histories ('Little Hans' and the 'Rat Man' *Standard Edition* X:1-150.

——. (1910). Leonardo Da Vinci and a Memory of his Childhood,.In Five Lectures on Psycho-Analysis, Leonardo da Vinci and Other Works, *Standard Edition* XI: 57-138.

——. (1913). On Beginning the Treatment (Further Recommendations on the Technique of Psycho-Analysis I*)*. In: The Case of Schreber, Papers on Technique and Other Works *Standard Edition* XII:121-144.

——. (1914). Remembering, Repeating and Working-Through (Further Recommendations on the Technique of Psycho-Analysis II*)*. In: The Case of Schreber, Papers on Technique and Other Works *Standard Edition* XII:145-156.

——. (1915). Observations on Transference-Love (Further Recommendations on the Technique of Psycho-Analysis III). *)*. In: The Case of Schreber, Papers on Technique and Other Works *Standard Edition* XII:157-171.

——. (1920). Beyond the Pleasure Principle. In: Beyond the Pleasure Principle, Group Psychology and Other Works *Standard Edition* XVIII 1-64.

——. (1923). The Ego and the Id. *Standard Edition* XIX:1-66.

——. (1926). Inhibitions, Symptoms and Anxiety. In: An Autobiographical Study, Inhibitions, Symptoms and Anxiety, The Question of Lay Analysis and Other Works. *Standard Edition* XX: 75-176.

Jones, E. (1949). *Hamlet and Oedipus.* London: V. Gollancz..

Klein, M. (1950). On the Criteria for the Termination of a Psycho-Analysis. *International Journal of Psycho-Analysis* 31:78-80.

——. (1950). On the Criteria for the Termination of an Analysis. *International Journal of Psycho-Analysis* 31:204-204.

www.ingramcontent.com/pod-product-compliance
Lightning Source LLC
Chambersburg PA
CBHW072154020426
42334CB00018B/1997